I REMEMBER CHESTERFIELD

I REMEMBER
CHESTERFIELD
A MEMOIR

Micki Savin

Copyright 2005 by Micki Savin. All rights reserved.

No part of this book may be reproduced, stored in a retrieval system, or transmitted by any means, electronic, mechanical, photocopying, recording, or otherwise, without written permission from the author.

First published by AuthorHouse January, 2005

ISBN: 1-4184-5250-5 (e-book)
ISBN: 1-4184-5251-3 (Paperback)
ISBN: 1-4184-5249-1 (Dust Jacket)

Library of Congress Control Number: 2003099582

This book is printed on acid free paper.

Printed in the United States of America
AuthorHouse
www.authorhouse.com
Bloomington, IN

DEDICATION

I Remember Chesterfield, a personal memoir, is dedicated to the memory of my son, United States Air Force Lieutenant Mitchell Jay Savin, to my precious and loving daughter Nancy whose constant encouragement inspired the writing of this book and to my cherished son David, whose love sustains me.

ACKNOWLEDGMENTS

I am grateful to former Radcliffe Writing Institute Professor Gail Pool and her writing class, and especially Electa Kane Tritsch, for their interest and guidance; to my daughter Nancy R. Savin for her dedication in editing this book for publication, to Sandra Kersten Chalk for her devoted assistance in preparing the manuscript, to my cousin Bernard Saul for substantiating my remembrances, to Dr. Bernard Wax for his careful reading of the manuscript, to my grandaughter Yohanna Willheim for her assistance with the production of the images and the map of Chesterfield, to Miranda Johns and Kyiesha Isiah of AuthorHouse for their guidance, and to all who kindly loaned their dear pictures including Montville town historian Jon Chase.

CONTENTS

INTRODUCTION xi

PART I 1887-1911

Chapter I	The Synagogue	1
Chapter II	Chesterfield – A *Shtetl* in America	10
Chapter III	Baron Maurice de Hirsch	22
Chapter IV	… And So We Came to Chesterfield	34
Chapter V	The Two Weddings	39

PART II 1911-1932

Chapter VI	The Store	52
Chapter VII	Chesterfield As I First Knew It	67
Chapter VIII	The Farm	73
Chapter IX	The Accident	81
Chapter X	Halcyon Days in Chesterfield	87
Chapter XI	My Teens	94
Chapter XII	The Summer That Changed My Life	103
Chapter XIII	My Grandmother	117

PART III 1932-1982

Chapter XIV	The Transition	127
Chapter XV	My Grandfather	138
Chapter XVI	Mama	147
Chapter XVII	Mama's Properties	155
Chapter XVIII	Thanksgiving at Mama's	159
Chapter XIX	Mama and I	165
Chapter XX	I Find My Russian Roots	179
Chapter XXI	The Living End	195
Epilogue	The Monument	201
BIBLIOGRAPHY		205

INTRODUCTION

My maternal grandparents, John and Sarah Kaplan, arrived in New York City from Russia in December, 1887.

Three years later, they purchased a farm in Chesterfield, Connecticut, an agricultural community sponsored by the Baron Maurice de Hirsch. In a later chapter I shall discuss the Baron, a German industrialist of extraordinary wealth and philanthropy who helped resettle thousands of Eastern European Jewish immigrants across the United States in the late 19th century, my great-grand and grandparents among them.

Chesterfield is not where I grew up. We lived in Norwich, about 15 miles away, but I spent many, many happy days visiting my grandparents. I clearly remember their farm, the family, how they lived in this small farming community. With pleasure I recall swimming in Kosofski's delightful brook. Blueberrying in fragrant meadows. Grandpa's general store and dance hall. The austere little synagogue. I can never forget some of the residents. Isadore Savin whom I married and with whom I had a 40 year love affair. Mama, my most unusual mother-in-law, and this community of hard-working Russian Jewish immigrants who forged another way of life for the generations who followed.

This Chesterfield Jewish community has long perished. And when I, the oldest living grandchild of John and Sarah, shall die, all the wonderful memories I hold dear will pass away too. Time pushes my pen to write them down.

In 1998, at the age of 87, I was thrilled when Gail Pool, an English professor at Radcliffe College, Cambridge, Massachusetts, accepted me as a graduate student in her class "Writing for Publication". It was the last year she would be teaching.

"What will you write?" she asked me.

"A memoir," I answered her. "I remember Chesterfield."

Searching my memory has been an enthralling experience. I discovered Memory is a sometime thing. It pops up like a jack-in-the-box at the oddest times, anywhere. It surprised me, elated me. I hadn't expected to remember so much.

I found Memory to be a playful thing. It doesn't flow like a silent, underground stream of people and events. It jogs and twists, sometimes reverses and churns up pertinent details months later. I have had great fun with Memory.

But Memory also challenged me. Although I structured this book chronologically, I found gaps, overlaps and incidents difficult to place. Like Aunt Rose's wedding. She was married in 1909, but I didn't learn the wonderful details until 1984.

Some of the chapters are not strictly pure memoir. They contain historical material that occurred over 100 years ago which is vital to my story. History shaped the destinies of those people who chose to live in Chesterfield. It created the unique qualities that characterized Chesterfield. In turn, they became a part of me.

Besides, I was fascinated by the historic drama about which I had known nothing.

Micki Savin
Bloomfield, Connecticut, 2004

Chesterfield Synagogue, 1892

The Synagogue

Chapter I

In a whim of nostalgia, just before Mothers Day, 1977, I returned to Chesterfield. I heard that the little synagogue I once knew so well had burned down. Abandoned, because the community of immigrant Russian farmers who had worshipped there no longer existed, struck twice by lightning, assailed by vandals and now fire, the building finally succumbed.

Parking my car off the busy highway I pushed my way through the formerly familiar path, now hidden by thick, indiscriminate brush, and came out on the *shul* (synagogue) yard, a grassy knoll on the edge of a hillside. My eyes drank in the wide sweep of lush valley below where my grandfather's cows once grazed, their bells a faint melody in the summer breeze. In a dip of the land, before my time, had stood a small house for the *shoket* (ritual slaughterer) and the *mikvah* (ritual women's bath). Ahead of me, at the far end of the clearing, lay a few charred timbers scattered and desolate, all that remained of the once vibrant religious and social center the little synagogue had provided its congregants.

I noticed a man pushing a metal detector over the land, "What are you looking for?" I asked him.

"Coins. Old coins. You'd be surprised what I find in old church yards."

"You won't find any here," I told him. "These people were forbidden to carry any money on the Sabbath and Holy Days, and," I chuckled, "Who had any? They were so poor."

He believed me and left quietly. Alone, I stood in the damp May morning, in utter silence, memories crowding, tears unshed. All I had once loved was now gone.

I must have been about four or five years old, dressed in a stiffly starched frock beautifully embroidered by my mother's sister Goldie. On top of the thick black curls my mother so carefully shaped around her fingers, she had fastened a wide pink moiré ribbon with scalloped edges. My white shoes and high white socks were immaculate. This afternoon she was taking my sister Libby, equally starched and coiffured, and me to visit her parents who lived on their farm in Chesterfield. Though casual clothes would have been more appropriate, my mother's pride in dressing her girls was strong. I often think she fussed with us because we were the dolls she never had to play with when she was a child. And she looked beautiful for the trip, wearing a big brimmed hat and high buttoned shoes.

We lived in the Greeneville section of Norwich. At Franklin Square we boarded the summer trolley to Montville, about seven miles away. How I loved those summer trolleys! What an adventure it was to ride them. Highly polished yellow wooden benches stretched across the width from perilously unprotected, open sides. As the trolley swayed and raced on its tracks, the brush of summer heat fanned my eager face, thrilling me. Fascinated, I watched the intrepid conductor precariously propel himself along the outer step, thrusting his long pole in front of each bench so the passengers could drop their nickel fares in the receptacle dangling at the end. I was afraid he would fall off. The speed was exhilarating, and, thankfully, just as I began to be motion sick, we reached our stop.

I waved vigorously to my handsome Uncle Ben who was standing with his horse and buggy across the road. He hoisted me up onto the single seat and I sat between him and my mother. Libby, two years younger than I, sat primly on her lap.

The horse trotted toward Oakdale, a small town halfway to Chesterfield, and my mother pointed out Robertson's Box Factory. Once again we heard her story:

> When I was 13 and Rose was 14, we worked there from Monday through Saturday for $3 a week. $2.50 went for our room and board with a family in Oakdale and each weekend, when we walked the seven miles home, we gave Papa the much-needed fifty cents.

We soon turned north toward Chesterfield. The day was warm and cozy. We rode in dappled sunshine, a billow of dust pursuing us. When we came to a bleak, nondescript, gray building, my mother, who had a great sense of drama, explained that this was the Poor House where old people, who had no money, no one to care for them, and could no longer work, came to spend their last years. I remember this upset me. The place looked so grim and fearsome.

A few miles further and we approached the top of Chapel Hill. The horse, nearing home, picked up his pace and no matter how hard Uncle Ben tightened the reins, the beast scampered down the hill, nearly upsetting us as we bumped over "thank-you ma'ams." We crossed the main road and in minutes pulled up in front of the farmhouse. My grandmother stood on the porch of the summer kitchen. She bent to embrace us. She smelled so fresh and sweet,

I Remember Chesterfield

her skin so soft, like crushed rose petals. Her shiny black hair was twisted in a topknot, her housedress spotless.

గళ గళ

The memory faded ... vanished ... and I realized where I was. Crossing the diminished *shul* yard, standing near the burnt timbers, all I could see were the shrubs that had sprung up where the synagogue had been.

గళ గళ

I was 19, a junior at Connecticut College for Women in New London. I had chosen to spend the *Rosh Hashonah* holidays with my grandparents on the farm. I loved going there and being with them. Their hearts were full of love. They never scolded or preached or probed. They accepted me as I was and I loved them dearly.

They had gone early to the services at the little synagogue but I waited until late midmorning to join them. I felt so good that day. I wore a light knit yellow suit with a white blouse and full-length coat, my long black hair coiled in a low bun. I strolled down the short incline from the house, turned right onto a skinny, unpaved road, shadowed by maple trees whose just turning leaves arched overhead. Lush festoons of wild purple grapes hung in beautiful swags. In the ditches scarlet runners of poison ivy threatened all who dared to disturb them. Goldenrod, blue gentians and white asters bloomed profusely. The sky was sheer blue; the autumn air gentle

The Synagogue

and warm, perfumed by the scent of fallen apples decaying in a nearby orchard and the rich fragrance of hay stacks standing like silent giants in the newly mown meadows. I remember thinking Heaven must be like this.

Slowly I walked past a weathered wooden building on my left, half collapsed and reputed to have once been a Russian Orthodox Church. At the one-room schoolhouse on the corner I met the main road that had been paved after World War I. Because it ran from Hartford, the state capitol, to New London and the sea, it was called the Military Highway. Turning right on it, I wandered slowly past Miller's butcher shop and my grandfather's General Store, closed for the holidays. A short distance up the hill, onto the well-worn path, I came to the *shul* yard, a grassy clearing on the side of the hill. At the far end stood the synagogue, a one story box-like structure, maybe 38 by 45 feet, simple in design, pristine in white paint with green trim. Four large windows punctuated the north and south sides. In the recess created by an extended vestibule, a bare bench tipped back, holding a shiny bucket of sweet drinking water and a ladle. A couple of children played on the grass. Two men had come out for a break and from the open door I could hear the drone of muffled prayer. Leisurely crossing the small area I stopped to admire the lovely valley sweeping down to the right. Then, with a last deep breath of pure country air, I walked up the five uneven steps and paused in the double doorway. The scene, except for the shabby, lopsided dark green window shades, could have been the original one when the synagogue was dedicated in 1892, nearly 40 years before.

According to tradition, the synagogue faced East. A small, unassuming stained glass window crowned the Ark whose embroidered black velvet curtain, donated by my grandparents John and Sarah Kaplan, was drawn to display the extra *Torahs* (Old Testament). Perpendicular to the side walls were a dozen or so pews, painted a dull brown. In a rear pew a few prayer books lay haphazard. Near the door, the black potbellied stove was unlit. And in the center of the building stood the *bema,* (Greek for raised platform) on which was spread an opened *Torah*. The men, heads and bodies wrapped in voluminous prayer shawls, were praying as if each one's fate depended upon the loudness and fervor of their requests to God. To the left a long, faded green curtain separated the women from the men. I slipped behind it and found a seat next to my grandmother.

    Bitter as gall had been the existence of the women around me but on this day, their arduous holiday chores behind them, they came to thank the Almighty for their blessings. An occasional new hat or scarf some fond daughter had sent brightened their faded finery. Bent over, their tired, aged bodies exhausted from child bearing and endless labor, hands gnarled and swollen, they rocked as they prayed and wept for the ones they lost. And when their moaning reached a crescendo, Mr. Miller, a butcher by trade, a small man who had sired six daughters and then a son, banged on the *bema* and shouted, *"Sha, Vybe, Sha."* (Be quiet, women, be quiet.)

    As I sat there, understanding little and unable to read the Hebrew, I tried to imagine the beginnings of this small community. I was surprised by how little I knew. What role did my great grandfather, Harris Kaplan, play in erecting this building, so vital to the community? How did these people come together in this small, rural Connecticut village, far from their homeland and native culture?

The Synagogue

I could visualize the past thanksgiving joys of *Succoth* when the congregants adorned their outside shelters with the fruits of the harvest and rejoiced in its abundance. Dancing at *Simchas Torah*. Celebrating a *Bar Mitzvah*, a young boy's coming into manhood. The naming of a new baby. A bridegroom being called to the Torah and then being pelted with raisins. These people had overcome the starkness and poverty, the struggle outside. In this simple little shul the shared intimacy of their devout worship of God, the absence of oppression and fear enriched the congregants' lives. But I had never wondered how or why it all began.

As I sat there I found myself getting restless. The sobbing affected me. The air was stifling. What am I doing here I asked myself. I'm not like these people. My life will be different. I'm too young, too educated, too full of promise. Once they were too, but times have changed. Telling my grandmother I'd see her later, I left.

As I came down into the yard, Isi, the youngest Savin son, followed me.

"Happy New Year, Micki," he said.

"Happy New Year too," I answered.

"I'm glad to see you. How are you?"

"I'm fine, thanks. How are you?"

"I'm good, thank you. Why are you leaving?"

"I just couldn't take anymore, It's so hot in there and no one would dare open a window. Somebody would surely complain of a draft." I knew I was annoyed and critical. "And the services are not for me. I don't understand the Hebrew and the Cantor's not so great. Usually I like music."

I Remember Chesterfield

"Well," he laughed, "they bring in someone from New York for whatever they can afford to pay. They're just glad to get a Cantor."

"I'm just impatient, I guess." I started to walk away.

"Where are you going?"

"Back to the farm."

"I'll walk with you."

Little did I ever dream that in two years Isi and I would be married.

Now he was gone. I stood there, charred timbers at my feet, relics of all that once had been so wonderful. A damp breeze rose and blew through the emptiness. No one remained. The descendants had all moved away, merging into America from coast to coast. Solemnly, I walked back to my car through the rampant brush, under the branches of a wild dogwood tree in bloom.

May the souls of the departed rest in peace.

The Synagogue

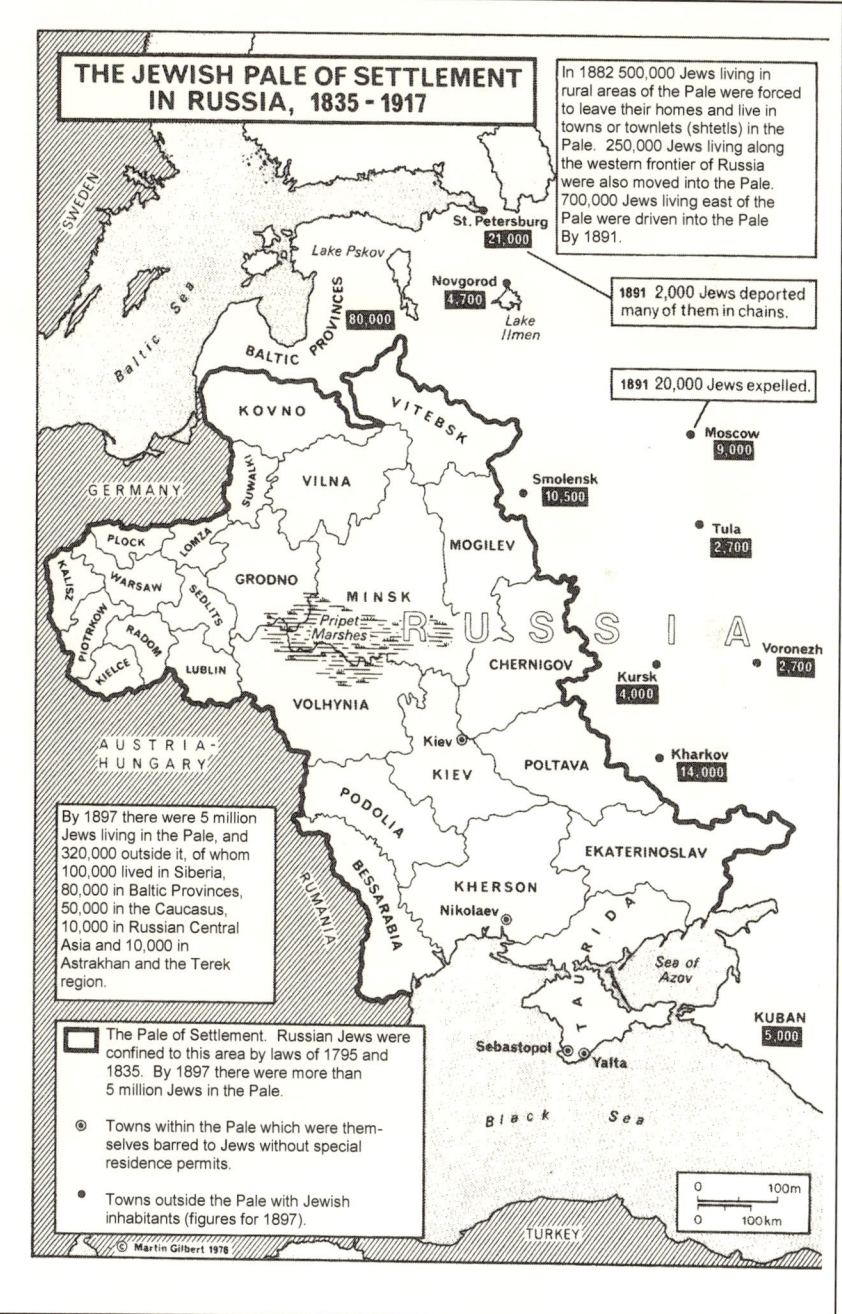

The Jewish Pale of Settlement in Russia, 1835 - 1917 © Martin Gilbert, The Routledge Atlas of Jewish History, 6th Edition By Martin Gilbert.

Chesterfield – A *Shtetl* in America
Chapter II

In the early 1890s, several years before I was born, Chesterfield, Connecticut was a cluster of small farms, bisected by a single dirt road that rolled north-northwest out of the environs of New London, Connecticut. For nine miles, the road (now Route 85) passed through a sparsely populated rural landscape, then plummeted down a long hill, leveled out, and a mile further, touched the Salem town line.

Just before the hill, the New London Reservoir, a lovely stretch of blue water circled by tall pines, created a picturesque view. My mother, who often related some of the hardships she and her siblings suffered, told me, "When I was growing up I'd go out at dawn to fish in the reservoir. It was illegal to do that and I was so scared I'd get caught, but we needed the fish. We were always hungry."

The area comprising Chesterfield, a section of the town of Montville, was not very big. It spread along the dirt road for four or five miles. How far back the boundaries on either side of the road extended could have been only a few miles. Within this limited stretch of land, agents of the Baron de Hirsch settled about thirty Russian Jewish immigrant families who desired to live in New England. Previous Yankee owners had abandoned the small farms purchased by the new settlers, 40 – 100 acres of land in poor condition. Neglected buildings in need of repair. The rocky and overgrown earth had to be cleared. But the price of $10 - $15 an acre was considered a bargain.

Chesterfield - A Shtetl in America

To qualify for acceptance, the future settlers were required to possess a working capital of at least $400 to $1,000. The Baron de Hirsch fund loaned them mortgage money and offered financial assistance for three years.

Between 1890 and 1895 several families came to Chesterfield under the Baron's auspices but soon moved on to more profitable and easier avenues of success. There was a rapid turnover of properties. The 30 or so steadfast families who persisted and took root in Chesterfield endured great poverty. I knew many of them and their descendents: the Schneiders, Gruskins, Leviloffs, Cohens, Millers, Savins, the John, Issac and Yale Kaplan families, Agranovitchs, and the Polskys.

And they struggled. Alien to the land, alien to the language, alien to the customs, they created their own village, a *shtetl*, similar to which they were accustomed. There was a blacksmith, a cobbler, a Hebrew teacher, a synagogue, a bakery and a cemetery. Although the families had come from diverse localities in Russia, their shared culture formed a cohesive community among their Yankee neighbors.

The farms were meager, the soil tired from years of previous cultivation. Unfortunately, any knowledge of farming had not been a prerequisite for the people who settled on this land. Farming was slow and ungainful. The salt of human sweat seasoned the piles of hay stacked high in the fragrant meadows. It poured onto the long hills of potatoes, cabbage and fodder raised against a relentless winter. It froze as the men made their way to steamy barns on icy mornings. It stained their clothes, seared their lives as they unceasingly wrestled with the barren, stony soil of New England. Dairy farming was popular and the

I Remember Chesterfield

The Chesterfield Creamery

Postcard of Main Street, Chesterfield, c. 1910

Chesterfield's one-room schoolhouse

farmers by building a Creamery on Flanders Road. Here the farmers could sell their milk for a penny or two a quart to the New London Dairy. However, the cows, usually a herd consisting of a dozen animals, were of mediocre quality and did not produce adequately.

The children came fast, almost one a year. Into the one room schoolhouse they crowded and learned to speak English, properly pronounced, which they taught to their parents. They learned reading, writing and arithmetic, a little American history and the strange story of Christmas.

As the end of the century neared, circumstances improved. Some of the farmers began to take summer paying guests. Called "pleasurefolk," they came from the teeming neighborhoods of New York City to escape the dreaded heat and to avoid the childhood diseases. Mumps, measles, chicken pox, poliomyelitis, whooping cough, scarlet fever, diphtheria, violent, rampant and uncontrolled, exacted a fatal toll.

Jewish boarders flocked to Chesterfield. They expected to gain 20 pounds a summer on the unpolluted air and the excellent, ample cuisine prepared by the farmers' wives. I remember my cousin Ethel telling me that she had seen my grandmother cooking on four wood-burning stoves simultaneously for the many guests staying at the farm. Corpulence was a symbol of success. It indicated that a person possessed enough money to buy food. Fancy accommodations were unimportant. People slept two or three to a bed, often three beds to a room. They bathed in the brooks and in the evenings created their own entertainment. Someone played the piano. They danced and sang and kibitzed. At one farm a mock marriage was presented. The bride was wrapped in shawls and veils, but not pretty. She had no dowry and this created much merriment. Some spectators were really fooled until, when the ceremony was over, the bride turned out to be Moe Savin.

Boarders were well pleased in Chesterfield. They enjoyed being in a comparable Jewish enclave, feasted each day on three whopping big meals, a generous teatime and a satisfying snack before going to bed. All for $1.00 a day for each person.

The following would be a typical day's menu:

BREAKFAST 8:00 AM
    Fruit
    Cereal, hot or cold
    Eggs, cooked to order, any style
    Herring, fried, plain or pickled
    Farmers cheese, blueberries or bananas, clotted cream
    Pancakes, French toast, or coffee cake

Bread, butter, jelly
　　　Coffee cake
　　　Pitchers of fresh milk, sweet cream, coffee, cocoa

DINNER 12:30 PM
　　　Appetizer such as chopped liver or *fricassee*
　　　Hot soup with accompaniments
　　　Roast meat or chicken, potatoes, noodle pudding, *tzimmes*, (carrots and sweet potatoes) peas or string beans
　　　Dill pickles or applesauce
　　　Dessert, usually fruit compote or pie

TEA 4:00 PM
　　　Tea, cake, strudel, cookies, preserves

SUPPER 6:00 PM
　　　Cold soup, borscht or schav
　　　Fried fish or canned salmon
　　　Corn on the cob
　　　Blueberries, farmer cheese, clotted cream
　　　Sliced tomato, cucumbers
　　　Dessert, rice pudding
　　　Pitchers of milk, sweet cream, coffee

At bedtime there was always a snack lest anyone get hungry in the night. All one could eat. All dairy products home made. All vegetables from the garden. All prepared on slow wood-fired stoves in the summer kitchens.

The heyday of Chesterfield boarders probably lasted from 1895 to 1915 when the Creamery closed. I remember my mother-in-law kept a few boarders, old friends, as late as 1930. Families did continue to come to Chesterfield as independent roomers. They were different from the earlier boarders. They rented one or two rooms for the summer, usually unoccupied spare bedrooms, with cooking privileges. This was an advantage for both the farmers and the visitors. From the host farmers they bought milk, eggs, butter,

I Remember Chesterfield

cheese, chicken, fresh vegetables. Peddlers drove into the farmers' yards to sell fruit, fish and fresh baked goods. Mr. Miller sold meat and my grandfather's store offered other supplies.

As I write about the boarders and roomers, I am reminded of the time I went to visit my mother's cousin, Lou Kaplan, who was wintering at the Palm Beach Spa. As we were chatting, into the main dining room the vacationers streamed and took seats. Waiters carried in trays of finger sandwiches, assorted cookies, strudel, brownies, decorated cakes, cheese, crackers, preserves, fruit squares, miniature eclairs. I chuckled to Lou as I looked around; "Looks like what Chesterfield must have been when there were boarders."

"Yeah," he said dryly. "All that's missing is the flies."

How well I remember the flies in my grandparents' large summer dining room! There were coils of yellow sticky flypaper suspended from the ceiling light bulbs, the frantic hiss of a fly caught on one. How we ducked not to get our hair caught. On the long tables sat open bowls of water, gray with sheets of black poisoned paper to lure the flies. Even though the barn and hencoop were at a considerable distance from the house and the opened windows were screened, the flies were attracted by the aromas of food. They thronged through the open doors.

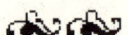

One of the intriguing features I remember about Chesterfield was the obvious absence of anti-Semitism. The Jewish people living in Chesterfield had come from widespread areas of Russia. All had known anti-Semitism and persecution as a way of life. Yet, despite the insulating aspects of the *shtetl*, they enjoyed a good relationship with their Yankee neighbors. A quote from the New London Day reporting a Chesterfield fire substantiates this fact:

> The Hebrews turned out and worked like beavers to help save some things from the burning buildings. The Chesterfield people speak in the highest terms of their Jewish neighbors who they say are industrious and orderly and mind their own business.

And I remember Isi telling me once, "I went to school with Christian boys and girls. We all sang the hymns and went to parties together. I didn't know any anti-Semitism until I got to Bulkeley High School in New London."

I close this chapter on the early settlement of Jewish people in Chesterfield with a story strong in my memory, one typewritten page of paper dear to my heart.

Midway during World War II, probably 1943, my brother-in-law, Butch Savin was awarded a contract to build fortifications on Fisher's Island, eight miles beyond the harbor of New London. These fortifications were designed to protect the highly vulnerable Thames

I Remember Chesterfield

River harbor area housing The United States Submarine Base, the Coast Guard Academy and Electric Boat Company where submarines are still being built. All people working on the job, including Isi, who worked for Butch, had to prove their U.S. citizenship. Imagine Isi's surprise when he went to Montville for a copy of his birth certificate. He discovered his birth on June 10, 1909 had never been recorded. It really isn't hard to understand, I presume Mama didn't realize she had to report the birth, nor did she have a doctor attend her at home. Also, the coming summer "season" was upon her and preparations for the summer guests were very much her full responsibility.

The Montville Registrar, whose name is no longer legible on the paper, wrote:

> I feel it is also worthwhile to note some of the background of this belated registration of birth, since it pertains to a sizable group of individuals born in the Town of Montville during the early part of this century.
>
> Around 1889 – 1900, Baron de Hirsch, a wealthy German-Jewish industrialist, sought to improve the lives of Russian and Lithuanian Jews. He arranged for quite a large number of families to migrate to this country and be settled in colonies. One of these colonies was in Chesterfield, Connecticut, in the Town of Montville. To the best of my knowledge, two other colonies were located in or near Vineland, New Jersey and Cayuga Lake, New York. It was the Baron's intention for these families to become farmers, which they did, at least for one generation.
>
> Needless to say, because these people were living in a colony of their own people, that first generation in this country did not speak English very well; therefore their births, when recorded, are frequently misspelled, or wrong dates given, doubtless because of the language barrier.

The offspring of these farmers have gone forth to become business and professional people of considerable stature in the area and the state. Many of them have belated birth registrations on record in Montville. They were recorded strictly in accordance with the Statutes of the State of Connecticut, and I am somewhat indignant that these people should be subjected to questioning as to the validity of something which was completely beyond their control.
THIS IS TO CERTIFY that the above and foregoing information is true and accurate to the best of my knowledge and belief.

I kept this smudged piece of paper all these years because I too felt the Clerk's indignation and understanding. I also realize her note was a great and justly deserved tribute to the Jewish settlers of Chesterfield, so many of whom I knew and loved.

Baron Maurice de Hirsch auf Gereuth (1831 - 1896) *Harper's Weekly*, c. 1890. Reproduced with permission of the Picture Collection of the New York Public Library

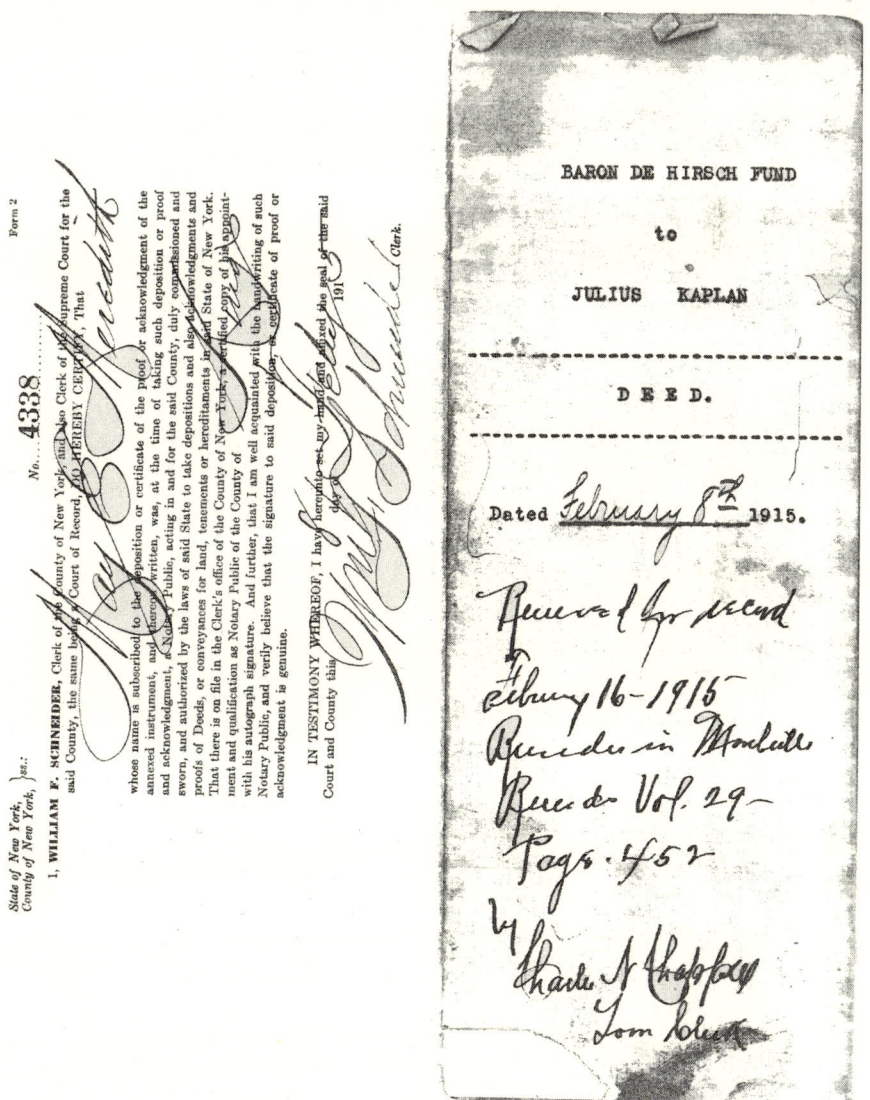

Baron de Hirsch Fund deed to Julius Kaplan, 1915

Baron Maurice de Hirsch

Chapter III

Not once during any of my short or extended visits to Chesterfield did I ever hear anyone allude to the Baron Maurice de Hirsch. He isn't well known in America despite the magnificently philanthropic role he played in the late 19th century when he assisted thousands of Russian Jewish refugees to find homes and financial independence in the United States, Canada and Argentina. Even my grandfather, who had lived through turbulent times in Russia and who had bought his farm in Chesterfield with the Baron's support, never spoke of his benefactor to me. The only thing he ever said, when I once asked him, was that he had come to America in the year of the big blizzard ... all else he knew of the past was lost years ago.

However, Baron Maurice de Hirsch deserves considerable mention. He was an heir of the brilliant, history-making Hirsch family.

Moses Hirsch von Gau-Konigshofer, Maurice's great grandfather, was the first Jewish person permitted to own land in Bavaria.

Moses' son, Jacob von Hirsch, Maurice's grandfather, was a learned Hebrew scholar as well as an exceptionally astute trader. His unusual financial prowess, major commercial successes and accumulation of great riches caught the attention of Maximillan Joseph. He appointed Jacob Court Banker to the Bavarian Crown.

This tenuous position afforded Jacob many privileges and advantages. In the War of Liberation (1815–1818) Jacob assembled and equipped a regiment of soldiers which he offered to the Bavarian armed forces. They helped defeat Napoleon. For this superb gesture Jacob was raised to nobility by royal proclamation on August 13, 1818. Baron Jacob von Hirsch became the first Jew in Bavaria allowed to engage in agricultural pursuits. In his lifetime, Jacob laid the foundations of phenomenal wealth for his descendants.

Baron Joseph von Hirsch, Jacob's son and Maurice's father, also a banker and a builder of railroads, married Caroline Wertheimer, thus adding the power, prestige and influence of her long distinguished family to the vast fortunes of the Hirsch family. Caroline, who believed in the traditions of Judaism, taught by example the responsibility of moneyed people to help poor, underprivileged, needy people, especially their fellowmen in the ghettoes.

Born December 9, 1831, their third child, Baron Maurice de Hirsch was restless, a poor student and exhibited no special talent except for an early interest in and a flair for banking.

In 1844, at the age of 14, his parents sent him to Brussels, a more progressive, liberal and sophisticated city than Munich where the family lived. At *l'Ecole Centrale des Arts et Manufactures,* in addition to his native German, Maurice learned fluent French and English. He acquired social graces such as riding and dancing, a knowledgeable conversation about the Arts and an air of refinement.

At seventeen, young, wealthy, adventurous and brash, he entered the prestigious banking firm of Bischoffsheim und Goldschmidt. Raphael Bischoffsheim was a close friend of Maurice's

I Remember Chesterfield

father. Here Maurice met and on June 28, 1855 married Clara Bischoffsheim in a most lavish wedding that united two banking fortunes.

Blessed with gifts of facile communication, a flair for statesmanship and a list of influential friends he cultivated, the Baron mingled early and easily in high society. In his photograph he presents an image of a tall, handsome, dashing aristocrat.

The Baron gained his own fame and fortune when he conceived the brilliant idea of building a railroad from Vienna to Constantinople so that the vast riches of the Middle East could more readily reach the hungry markets of Europe. However, no individual, moneyed entrepreneur or prosperous bank would invest in his scheme. Not daunted, the Baron finally convinced the Sultan of the Ottoman Empire to finance the construction of the railroad from Constantinople westward. In 1888, with great acclaim and celebration, the Orient Express was completed. Baron Maurice de Hirsch became one of Europe's richest men and outstanding philanthropists of the 19th century.

During the several years it took to negotiate and build this sprawling railroad Maurice and Clara had many times traversed the wide open stretches and cities of Poland, Galicia, the Balkans and Russia, nations that held the Jewish population (5,000,000 in the Russian Pale of Settlement alone), in the most sordid, deplorable and oppressed conditions. He witnessed the pitiful plight of the Jews and vowed to rescue them. At first he offered the Russian government a financial grant of 50 million francs, but Russia, willing to accept the money, would not promise to alleviate the living conditions of the Jewish people.

After their son Lucien, their only child, died in 1888 the Baron and Baroness turned all their attention to dispersing their fortunes for charitable purposes. "My son I have lost, but not my heir. Humanity is my heir," de Hirsch wrote.

Influenced by his mother's teachings, to always help the long suffering and less fortunate Jewish people of the ghetto, the Baron believed it was his God-given destiny to save these people, to move them out of Eastern Europe.[1] He sent scouts into the world to find countries with suitable land, willing to accept the immigrants and provide the best advantages. The ownership of land was vital in the Baron's philosophy. He thought the immigrants would be content in agriculture, farming as their Biblical ancestors had done. But not in Palestine. He decided Palestine was a disease-infested country, barren and desolate, no place for resettlement. This feeling persisted despite the growing movement inspired by Theodor Herzl that the time had come for Jews to return to Palestine and establish a Jewish homeland there. Furthermore, the Baron assumed that Russia would soon usurp the area.

Both Clara and Maurice were convinced that charity should not be an ongoing dole but should be given to assist the people to

---

[1] "What I desire to accomplish, what after many failures has come to be the object of my life and that for which I am ready to stake my wealth and my intellectual powers, is to give a portion of my companions in faith the possibility of finding a new existence, primarily as farmers and also as handicraftsmen, in those lands where the laws and religious tolerance permit them to carry on the struggle for existence as noble and responsible subjects of a humane government. Baron Maurice de Hirsch (1831 - 1896). *Moses of the New World,* Samuel J. Lee, page 214.

become self-supporting. To this cause they devoted the rest of their lives.

On February 9, 1891, Baron Maurice de Hirsch established an American de Hirsch Fund with $2,400,000 in New York City, incorporated under the laws of New York State. The purpose of this endowment was to administer moneys needed for the tremendous migration and resettlement of Jews that he envisioned. Colonies were established in Western Canada and across the United States, several concentrated in New England and the Mid-Atlantic States.

In Connecticut there were three Baron de Hirsch communities, Ellington, Colchester and Chesterfield. My grandparents, John and Sarah Kaplan, their seven children, his parents, and other close relatives lived in Chesterfield.

I was over sixty years old when I first heard about Baron Maurice de Hirsch, the gigantic migration of East European Jewish people from 1881 to 1914 and the numerous colonies the Baron sponsored for them. I had never really known what great catastrophe compelled millions to desert their homeland. After all, Jews had lived in Russia for 500 years. I also realized I had never stopped to question my own forebears about why they came to this country or from where in Russia they had escaped.

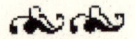

As I look back, I remember hearing how harrowing had been my mother-in-law's trip in 1891 when she fled from the Pale of Settlement with her brother Wolf, who could no longer evade conscription into the Russian army.

I also remember vaguely that when I was a child in Chesterfield, now and then I'd overhear some adult roomer chatting in the summer dining room say, "*A klug tsu Columbus.*" Spoken disdainfully. What was a *"klug?"* A plague? A deprecation? A banishment? I knew it wasn't anything good.

Years later, when I happened to be in New York at the YIVO, a library where Jewish archives are stored, I found the answer to these questions. To my great amusement I read that so many Russian Jewish immigrants, desperately seasick as they crossed the Atlantic in the stinking, crowded, abysmal conditions of steerage, were furious and so disgusted with Columbus because he had discovered America. If he hadn't, they argued, they would never be in such misery, a willing-to-die predicament. "A klug (a pox) to you, Columbus."

While I was writing this chapter my Memory gave me another happy jolt. It spewed forth the only story my father ever told us about his childhood in what is now Lithuania.

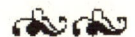

I Remember Chesterfield

Father, Libby and Micki at the Greeneville Grain Company

Baron Maurice de Hirsch

Micki, age 6 months

Micki holding *The Kodakery*

I Remember Chesterfield

We were living in Greeneville at the time where my father owned a grain store on North Main Street. In the winter the building was unheated. He would come home chilled. I can visualize our little kitchen. After supper he was wont to pull up a chair close to the stove, put his stockinged feet in the lingering warmth of the oven – the fire had been banked – take Libby on one knee, me on the other. This was his special time with his girls. I was still young enough to sit on his lap. He must have been in a rare mood of reminiscence that evening. I can remember how softly he spoke:

> "My mother had bought me a new pair of shoes," he said. "I was so pleased I tied the laces together and carried them around my neck. I wouldn't wear them, even though I had to cross a field where the grain had just been cut. My bare feet bled, but my shoes were too precious to put on."

And then another story, long forgotten, came to the surface. I was at a wedding of a distant cousin on my father's side when his cousin Jake Savage, whom I had not seen since 1927, approached me and greeted me warmly.

> "I remember your father Moshe well," he said and began to cry. "I was 15 years old, and just wandering around the streets when Moshe met me."
> "What are you doing with yourself, Yankel?" he asked.
> "Nothing. There's nothing to do."
> "So, come to America with me."
> Tears flowed down his face. "He took me, brought me over and cared for me all his life."

What could I say while I watched this elderly man sob as he recalled my father's kindness and his own deliverance? I stood there and I wondered, which young man, my father was only 20, about to migrate to a strange country, not knowing the language and pitfalls ahead, would assume the responsibility for another, younger person. When Jake finally wiped his tears I said, "Yes, my father was a caring person. And I remember how fond he was of you."

Once the page to the Baron de Hirsch saga was opened, I was eager to learn more about that particular time in history and more about Chesterfield.

I knew nothing about pogroms. They were far distant and bad. Evil. No one I ever knew or heard of referred to the unspeakable horrors of these outrages. Nor did I ever hear anyone actually speak of or bemoan the brutal difficulties of the long ocean voyage. No one was alive whom I could ask. And no Chesterfield descendant knew any more than I did. It was as though a wall of steel had slammed shut behind everyone who had immigrated and silence prevailed.

Fortunately for me, about that time Trinity College in Hartford, Connecticut where I had earned my masters degree, offered a fascinating seminar on the Soviet Union. I remember an extraordinary slide presentation of wonderful Russian paintings and their relation to the political history of the country beginning about the 12th century. I was thrilled as I listened to Professor Samuel Kassow, a brilliant lecturer when he spoke on the Soviet's past and current conditions. In particular, I remember an impassioned Russian-born poetess, pouring out her hopes and longings, as she recited her stirring plea to Mother Russia. I was so completely immersed in

I Remember Chesterfield

Russian culture I thought all that was missing was the blinis, caviar and vodka.

And I read a lot. Whatever I could find on Russia in the late 19th century.

Thus it was with great excitement and gratification that I discovered the historical events that forever changed the destiny of those emigrating Russian Jews. The assassination of Tsar Alexander II and the pogroms. I could easily conjure these scenes:

On March 1, 1881, a fine day in St. Petersburg, Tsar Alexander II and his splendid entourage are riding along Catherine Canal. Brilliant sunshine. Handsome horses prancing, plumes waving, harness bells ringing, lookers-on cheering. Suddenly from the crowd a bomb aimed at the Tsar flies and misses. Immediately the cavalcade halts. The Tsar steps down from his carriage.

"Thank God," he says to his officer, "You're not hurt."

"It's too early to thank God," Ignatius Grinevitski shouts as he flings a second bomb. It hits its target and all blows up in bits.

With the name of Ignatius, he would not be Jewish. He may have been a member of the People's Party who was demanding more reforms from the Tsar.

So frightened was the timid heir, Tsar Alexander III, he refused to have a public coronation. He ordered his Chief of Police, Pobydonostzev, known for his cruelty and mercilessness, to hunt down the culprits and destroy them. Jews were the natural scapegoat, mainly because they were stubborn and refused to convert to Christianity, although the inducements and rewards were many and magnificent.

Thus began the infamous pogroms. The first one erupted in 1881 at Elizabethgrad and spread rapidly. A band of fearsome Cossacks on horseback would ride into a Jewish enclave, sabers bared. Slash anything, anybody in their path. Maim, murder, burn, rape, loot, even kidnapping boys to serve as menials in the Russian army. So many Jews (65,000) fled the first year that the Russian government in May 1882 passed laws forbidding Jews to emigrate. Nevertheless, Jews still fled for their lives. Fear of the pogroms drove them. Using bribery and forged papers, they escaped to friendly, safe countries like Germany and England where agents of the Baron Maurice de Hirsch helped the refugees toward their final goal.

And so they came, unskilled, many of them penniless, ignorant of the hardships they would face. They came to America, the intrepid, the strong, the creative and adventurous. They settled in a country that welcomed them and in time they found peace and prosperity.

Like Chesterfield. Like my grandparents.

So unsuccessful were Russia's May 1882 laws they were rescinded ten years later, and the flood of immigration the Baron had foreseen began in earnest.

... And So We Came to Chesterfield
Chapter IV

Rummaging in the red box of my treasured mementos for pictures I wanted to use in this book, I discovered to my delight a folded sheet of yellowed paper, the penciled handwriting barely legible. The moment I opened it my Memory swung back to 1934, the summer my husband Isi, baby Mitchell, and I were temporarily living in Westerly, Rhode Island where he was working on a road construction job nearby. Aunt Esther, Grandpa's youngest sister, resided in Westerly, on Canal Street, in a humble apartment behind her husband's store.

She was a lovely woman. Despite the bitter tragedy of losing two beautiful young daughters because of cancer, she had a positive, rather jolly disposition. At 49, only 4 years older than my mother, her dark curly hair had not yet turned gray and on her pretty round face she wore unrimmed glasses. Genial and hospitable, she smiled easily. I spent many an enjoyable afternoon with her and her daughter Victoria that summer.

One day I must have asked her why the Kaplan family settled in Chesterfield. She was glad to answer me and as she spoke Victoria scribbled her words on the piece of paper I now held in my hand. The comments in brackets are mine.

...And So We Came to Chesterfield

She spoke:

> We came to America in December 1887. I was 2 years old. [She made no mention of how rough the voyage must have been or where they sailed from, or how the family escaped.]
>
> Papa, [Harris Kaplan, my great grandfather] and Mama [Vigassah Leah], my oldest brother John, 21, [my grandfather] with his bride Sarah 18, another brother Yale with his bride Mima, my two older sisters and I. Brothers Max and Isaac came later.
>
> [When they arrived in New York] Five dollars was all the money Papa had left. Everyone was hungry. [Pious people like Harris, respecting the Jewish dietary laws, embarked with presumably enough food for the three week journey.] At the suggestion of Papa's friend, Sophie Krim, [he may have met her on the ship] we went to Brooklyn where we lived for 3 years on Moore Street.
>
> Papa found employment peddling and installing panes of window glass, but he didn't like it. Such dirty work he felt was beneath his dignity. He was poetic. [I remember Aunt Esther groped for the word "poetic". She wasn't sure how to describe her father. Different? Above average? Romantic? Idealistic?] He got another job as a presser in a pants factory. Still he wasn't happy. Papa had studied at the famous *Yeshiva* [a Hebrew university] in Bialystok which was an honor for him. Educated as he was, he had difficulty learning English. He was embarrassed in his conversations. People laughed at him, mocked him. Another friend, Max Polsky, [who later lived in Chesterfield] advised Papa to contact the Baron de Hirsch offices that were operating in New York.
>
> And so we came to Chesterfield. All of Papa's eight children. [Joseph, I assume, was born in Brooklyn.] I was five years old and had to sleep on the floor. There was no bed for me.

Aunt Esther paused for a while. Her mood took on an aura of great pride:

I Remember Chesterfield

The day we moved to Chesterfield was a day of great rejoicing. While we were living in Brooklyn Papa had organized a Lubvitsher *Chevret* (a small, intimate group of worshippers allied with the Lubvitsher movement), and now the whole congregation celebrated with us in a grand sendoff. They were happy and singing as they marched with us all the way from the house to the pier. And, leading the procession was Papa, holding aloft a precious *Torah*.

I could envision my great grandfather Harris with his full white beard and forthright blue eyes aglow with religious fervor. In his exultant heart he must have cherished a dream of religious freedom as pure as that of the first Pilgrims.

Aunt Esther's last words were "Papa opened a pants factory in Chesterfield." Obviously, he was too old to choose to farm.

I never knew where Harris and his family lived. My grandfather, John, never spoke of him. My mother, born in 1890, was too young to remember him. I can only surmise that he purchased an abandoned homestead on Flanders Road, now Route 161. Here with the assistance of the Baron de Hirsch contacts he established his pants factory, an occupation he had experienced in Brooklyn. The building was the largest in the area and employed the most people. In those days, manufacturers in New York cut patterns of material, parceled them out to small factories where they were assembled and sewn, and then returned to New York to be pressed and sold. Goods for Harris's plant came to New London via the Fall River Steamship Line and were transported to Chesterfield by horse and wagon. The

Baron, true to his philosophy of enabling the immigrants to become financially independent, also helped establish other diverse factories in the areas close to Chesterfield like Uncasville and East Lyme.

Another reason I feel Harris lived on Flanders Road is that was where the little synagogue was situated. My patrician great grandfather, already recognized as a leader and religious organizer, would have called together the Jewish farmers to make plans for a house of worship. He would have donated the acre plus of his land for this purpose. The de Hirsch Foundation underwrote the project. Erected by the Ben and Rock Construction Company of New London at a cost of $900, the synagogue was dedicated on May 6, 1892. The congregants incorporated as the New England Hebrew Farmers of the Emanuel Society. As recorded in the Montville Town Records, their purpose and pledge was:

> We, the subscribers, for the purpose of perpetuating the cause of Judaism in all its essential purity, and cherishing and promoting its great and fundamental principles in the Rock upon which our undying Faith is founded, the belief in and worship of one God, hereby unite to form a Society for public worship according to the principles and practices of our Faith.

I possess the ledger containing the minutes of the synagogue's early years. Written so neatly and precisely in a fine Yiddish script, they detail the congregation's activities. Dues were a nickel a week.

For nearly 30 years the synagogue flourished, but as the older gentlemen died or moved away the *shul* was used less and less. Isi told me that while he was in high school on Saturdays he often was called to make the 10th man for a *minyan*, necessary to have a full service. Then the men, Isi laughed, would have a heated discussion whether it was more right for him to ride his bicycle (forbidden on the Sabbath) so they could participate in worship, or not hold a *minyan* if he didn't come. Later on the synagogue was opened only for the High Holy days when there would be enough men attending. Finally, in 1953, when my mother-in-law moved to live with her daughter Bess in New London, the building was closed. The sacred Torahs were donated to other places of worship.

As I close these few chapters about the Russian Jewish immigrants who became farmers in Chesterfield, I feel eminently satisfied. I have attempted to be more historically descriptive of the causes that sent the first settlers there, with a fuller portrayal of the Baron, his ancestors, philosophy and achievement in Chesterfield, and of course, my mother's people who chose to settle there.

This was my legacy, their gift to me.

The Two Weddings
Chapter V

Chronologically, the stories of the two weddings in Chesterfield, Aunt Rose's in 1909 and my mother's in 1910, belong in this part of the book. Yet, I didn't learn anything about them until decades later. Memory, my constant companion, and Imagination have served me well.

In 1984 my mother's younger brother, Uncle Jake, flew east from California where he had lived for several years. He came to visit his son Bobby who lived in New London, and us. It was a treat for me to see him on that hot Sunday afternoon in August when he and I sat alone on the front porch of my sister Libby's waterfront home at Crescent Beach. Eighty-five years young, Uncle Jake hadn't changed much. He had retained his smooth, good-looking face, neatly cut hair, trim, well-muscled body, the charm and the easy-going nonchalance he had always possessed. He took life as it comes.

A frisky breeze played over the sparkling blue water of Niantic Bay. As he rocked and relaxed in a big chair, Uncle Jake reminisced about the bygone days in Chesterfield. Suddenly he said, "You shud'a seen Rosie's wedding!" Rosie was the oldest of the five sisters and the first to be married. Immediately I was very interested. This was a story I hadn't heard before.

"I was 10 years old at the time." I could visualize him, a kid, the youngest of the siblings, goggle-eyed, grinning, excited at all the commotion, running errands, under everyone's foot.

"All the groom's family came from New York" [New York was the magic place.] "All of them," he went on. "They came by boat. Cost a dollar and a half then. If you wanted a stateroom cost another dollar." He laughed as he rocked slowly. "Nobody took a stateroom 'cause they docked in New London in the middle of the night, near the railroad station."

I remembered that old brick building (still standing) with its antique pull chain water closet.

"So they took over the place. Nobody else was around. They had their own liquor and musicians, so they drank and danced till it got light and we could come for them."

I could imagine the high spirits of those men and women off to the country for a good time, a wedding at that.

"That must have been some rollicking party," I agreed with him, but I was puzzled. "How did you get all those people out to the farm? It's nine miles from New London – they didn't walk."

"Naw," Uncle Jake was smiling as he rocked in his remembering. "Everyone who had a buggy or wagon donated it. Took two hours to get in and two hours back. Just like a parade."

I could imagine that string of assorted vehicles on a sweet summer morning, trailing the dusty road. And I could visualize the wedding ceremony out in the apple orchard, just beyond the house. The *chuppa* (wedding canopy) fluttering in the breeze, guests standing while the Rabbi intoned the seven blessings. The smashing of the glass. The joyous shouts of *mazeltov*. Good luck!

The Two Weddings

My Father, Morris Solomon, with his brother Simon

Then everyone moved into the summer dining room to drink, dance and enjoy my grandmother's delicious food. How good it was to meet each other, families, friends, neighbors and children. What a release from their daily toilsome tasks. The women in their high necked, long sleeved dresses sat together. They chatted and remembered their own weddings. The men danced with each other and remembered their youth.

"I bet the New Yorkers never had such a great time," I said to Uncle Jake.

"Great time?" Uncle Jake stopped rocking. He sat straight up and looked directly into my eyes. "A great time?" he repeated. "Why, instead of going home the next day, they had such a great time they stayed a whole week!"

My mother was married the following year on April 3, 1910. She never spoke about her wedding to me until, decades later, on a dark, sodden afternoon when she was visiting at our summer home.

I remember that afternoon well. A three day "line storm" had finally stopped raining. Through the front windows I could see the lingering grayness, the piles of wet seaweed scattered on the sand. Seagulls swirling overhead, shore birds skittering as they delighted in the seldom-washed-up delicacies. I had lit a fire in the big stone fireplace. The warmth was welcome. The mood mellow. In a cozy moment of rare intimacy between my mother and me I asked her, "How did you meet my father?" I had never known.

I was aware, though, that at twenty she was ten years younger than my father, Morris Jacob Solomon, who lived in Norwich, Connecticut. While I was growing up I knew very little about his

The Two Weddings

background except that he had emigrated from Russia in 1900, renounced his allegiance to Tsar Nicholas II four years later and became a United States citizen. He was the oldest of 13 children (nine survived) and the first of his family to come to this country. As soon as he was able he brought over his parents and eight siblings whom he supported until they could take care of themselves. He financed his brother Charles through University of Maryland Dental College.

In 1925 my father died. I was 13 years old. Two years later my mother Ida remarried and in her endeavor to create a new family, we seldom mentioned my father.

So it was not until several decades later that she told me the story of her wedding.

Mitchell, Micki, David and Nancy, 1944

I Remember Chesterfield

Now as I reminisce about this one conversation I want to digress to bask in the glow of gladsome memories that come to mind about the big, wonderful waterfront cottage I loved so well, and the happy, carefree hours Mitchell, Nancy, David and I spent there summer after summer.

In the fall of 1940 Nancy, our three-year-old daughter, developed a serious case of eczema. So bad was it that I finally took her to a well-reputed pediatrician in Boston who put her in the Childrens' Hospital. After 16 days Dr. Louis Webb Hill said to me, "She's proved negative to every test. Then he added, "If you can take her to the beach next summer it may help. Eczema patients seem to do better in the salt air."

So, in April, 1941 I went looking for a rental cottage but nothing seemed adequate until the agent drove me to Attawan Beach, a small curve in the Connecticut shore. Near Niantic, eight miles south of New London, the spacious cottage, built as a day cottage in 1900, stood on a lot measured from a butternut tree, long gone, to the high water mark. Dilapidated as it was, it possessed basic necessities: a bathtub, hot water when I lit the gas heater, an electric stove and an outside shower. It also harbored hundreds of dead flies piled against dirt streaked windows. Six inches of dust balls lay under the beds.

When I walked out and stood by myself in the thin April sunshine on the small stretch of sand, exhilaration raced through my blood. Inhaling the tangy salt breeze, gazing across the expanse of gentle blue water to the horizon and clear open sky, I fell in love with the place. Only a few houses occupied the five short blocks that counted as Attawan Beach. There would be plenty of room for the children to play and ride their bikes.

The cottage was for sale only.

We bought it for $2500 as it was. We scoured, cleaned, threw out, remodeled, modernized, painted, built a huge fireplace and a wide front porch, enclosed the shower and added a half bath room downstairs. I delighted in the square dining room table, the antique low, armless rocking chair, the four airy bedrooms.

Each summer, the day school closed I drove with the children to the beach and returned home to West Hartford the night before school opened.

Loving the long afternoons lolling on the sand, chatting with the neighbors, taking the last dip of the day in the cool invigorating sea, the hot shower, leisurely dinner, the informality, I was in my Heaven. The glory of it I never mentioned out loud, never confessed to anyone. No longer was I expected to spend the summer at Mama's in Chesterfield! They weren't bad or difficult, but now I had independence. And privacy. I could prepare the food I chose to eat.

Nancy's eczema cleared and never returned. Occasionally Isi would complain about the long commute but I didn't listen. He came whenever he could because we were where his heart lay. In later years he came every night.

My mother was quiet, slowly gathering her thoughts. I repeated, "How did you happen to marry my father?

I Remember Chesterfield

"Well," she answered me slowly, "he had been told there were pretty girls in Chesterfield. You see," she explained, "he waited until he was thirty years old, until his three older sisters, Eva, Dora and Rose were married before he looked for a wife. In those days it was a disgrace if a son married before the daughters. And so he went to Chesterfield. He was supposed to meet Cousin Molly, Uncle Yale's daughter, but he saw me and liked me."

My Mother, Ida Kaplan

The Two Weddings

No wonder, I thought. From her picture Ida was a beauty. Tall, slender (I remember how tight she laced her corsets), thick lustrous dark hair, clear skin, nice features and flirtatious eyes. Immaculate and attractively dressed as she always was.

"So he spoke to Grandpa." My mother was coy and wouldn't reveal much. "Arrangements were made and he gave Grandpa $200 for me to go to New York to buy furniture."

I doubted that matters had happened so quickly, but I knew that among religious Orthodox Jewish families like those in Chesterfield, marriages were arranged. Girls often had no choice, but my father was nice, nice looking, kind and generous.

"We set the date for April 3rd."

April ... the mating month. From down in the swamps rose the incessant shrill song of peep frogs. Spring, and the meadows were faint green. The pungent smell of damp earth upturned filled the air and the apple trees, too early for blossom, were swollen with young sap.

Guests, men, women, children had traveled over the muddy, deep-rutted lanes, fanned their wagons on the ground between the house and the sheds and tethered their horses. My father's well-to-do family came in two touring cars.

"Where did you hold the wedding?" I asked her. "It was too cold to be outside."

"In the summer dining room. Where else?"

"Did you have flowers?"

"Flowers?" She was indignant. "Who knew of such things? But Aunt Goldie and I scrubbed the room clean and Grandpa gave it a fresh coat of paint."

My mother must have looked elegant in the white satin gown with leg-of-mutton sleeves, a narrow waist and short train which her sister Rosie's husband, Louis, who worked in the needle trade, made. To it she pinned the diamond watch my father had given her.

What an affair that wedding must have been. People crowded into the room eating every last crumb my grandmother and the girls had cooked. The usual food: schnapps, wine, cellar fermented, *challah* over which to recite the blessings, herring and *kicklach*. Golden chicken soup with noodles and *mahndlen*, little nut-sized pieces of baked pastry dough. Crisp roasted chicken. Casseroles of long baked *tsimmes* (sweet potatoes and carrots, probably the last brought up from the winter cellar). Potato *kugels* and noodle puddings. All kinds of relishes. All manner of desserts: fruit compote, sponge cake, jellyroll, honey cake, mandelbread and poppy seed cookies.

And the dancing! Some local orchestra. Light hearted rhythmic music. Jewish and Russian dances familiar to the people. The handkerchief dance, the *kazatzka*, the *schirralla*, and the *hora*. I could picture my grandfather, hands clasped behind his back, his black rounded tip shoes taking tiny steps. He was always so light on his feet.

Merriment. Happiness. Gaiety. My parents' wedding was typical and traditional with one unusual occurrence. My great grandfather's dearest and closest friend, Hennoch Reitch, came with his daughter Sara Savin and her baby boy, Isadore, ten months old.

The Two Weddings

She was nursing him through the dangerous second summer. Now, when anyone asks me how I met my husband, I just smile and say, "I've always known him, he came to my mother's wedding."

※ ※

For a moment my mother and I sat silent, lost in our thoughts of long ago. Then she said sadly, "The 15 years I was married to your father were the best years of my life."

My heart plummeted. I was surprised she admitted that. I felt so sorry for her. What would she have been, I thought, if she had been given the education, advantages and privileges I had? Although born in Brooklyn in 1890, she was one of those persons lost in the transition and struggle of her parents from Russia to the small hamlet of Chesterfield. A meager grammar school education. Sent to work in a factory at 13. Furthermore, she was a victim of her times. A woman was expected to marry, wash, iron, and clean, cook, raise a family and stay at home. Which she did well. I remember in 1920 when Congress granted women the franchise to vote, my mother, in a burst of victory and celebration bobbed her beautiful black hair. My father was so upset about that he didn't speak to her for three days. She never cut it again.

She was always fearful of anything new or what she couldn't handle. Conditioned by fear – fear of hunger, fear of poverty, fear of her father's temper – and motivated by fear; she'd warn us … "if you are good, if you do the right thing, that bad thing won't happen. If you don't do this, something awful might come." … She existed within

I Remember Chesterfield

the narrow circle of her familiarity. Consequently she left me free to enter my fields of exploration. I learned early to make my own way.

I often argued with my mother. I was impatient with her until I accepted the truth that she would never, never change. And I learned. If a situation arose that she didn't want to face, she pawned it off on someone else, usually me.

Ida, I often called her that, had plenty of spirit and drive. She loved when people took us for sisters. People were always attracted to her. She was outstanding in her appearance and she possessed a charming personality. She was also a staunch Democrat. She taught me integrity and honesty.

But it was my father who taught us the rules of table etiquette, who set social standards of behavior for Libby and me. It was he who took care of us when we were sick, gave us our medicine and fed us. My father who bought me a Chickering baby grand piano for my ninth birthday. A gentle but firm man, highly principled, strongly moral, he tempered my mother's Chesterfield heritage with respect, love and innate good taste.

The Two Weddings

Libby, Father, Micki and the new Cadillac touring car, c. 1925

Chesterfield general store, c. 1950, rebuilt after it burned down in 1928

The Store
Chapter VI

I always loved going to Chesterfield to visit my grandparent's farm and store. After World War I my father had purchased a big, black Cadillac touring car and when the weather was favorable we drove out nearly every Sunday. I don't know if my mother felt it was her filial duty to go or she wanted a break from her daily routine or she really desired to see her folks, maybe all three.

I remember that car fondly. We sat high on tufted black leather seats. Two strong wires anchored the roof to the hood. Wide running boards stretched between oversized fenders. Glaring headlamps! And when it rained we snapped isinglass curtains into place. To start the car my father inserted a crank below the radiator. One ... two ... three quick turns and the ignition caught. Sometimes it took longer. When this happened I would wait tensely. I had heard that some men suffered broken arms doing this. But the pleasures the car brought have long lingered in my Memory.

⚜⚜

I recall the trip to Italy Isi and I took in 1967. Our guide in Sienna possessed an open touring car of similar vintage to my father's. On a beautiful Spring sunshiny afternoon we toured the charming old city, sitting tall on the black leather seats, top down, laughing and in high spirits. We watched college students in medieval costumes celebrate an historic event as they roamed and romped

The Store

through the narrow streets. I said to the guide, "My father had a car like this," and he answered me, "I bought it in 1914. The only reason I still have it is because when Mussolini confiscated all private cars I told him I needed this car to make a living. So he let me keep it."

Memory sidetracked me.

To get to Chesterfield from where we were living in Greeneville we did not take the sleepy, dusty dirt Oakdale Road over Chapel Hill, but drove roundabout to Montville and New London, then doubled back like a V. The road was wider and the drive took about an hour. Beyond New London, I remember there was a lulu of a treacherous spot, Douglas Hill. Today it is barely noticeable as a gentle rise, but at that time the ascent was sharp and steep. When it had rained, the hill, muddy, rutted and slippery, challenged the driver and the spinning tires as they fought for traction. The car groaned and swiveled crazily. We held our breaths until it finally crawled over the top and onto level ground.

Grandma's Sunday dinner was always the same. A delicious pot roast, long baked with crisp browned potatoes, dill pickles or sour green tomatoes that Grandpa had preserved in brine and spices.

Grandpa's store fascinated me. That's where the action was, but my Victorian father, born in 1880, never let me go down there by myself. He feared some farmhand, lounging about, would use language unfit for me to hear. Growing up, Libby and I had been very sheltered. No roller-skates, no ice skates, no bicycles. We might fall and get hurt. We played by ourselves in our backyard.

I Remember Chesterfield

While my father never said so, he considered the kids living in the vicinity roughnecks and unsuitable playmates. Greeneville was a mill town dominated by the United States Finishing Company that manufactured unbleached muslin. Most of the residents were immigrant families from Poland and Ireland and didn't speak English well.

There were only a few Jewish families in Greeneville. When I look back I understand how challenging and difficult it must have been for them to raise their children among Christians. When Christmas came with its bustle and festivities I remember how I envied and longed for a Christmas tree too. Out of the question. Yet my father let us hang our white stockings on the hot water pipes near the kitchen stove. On Christmas morning – at first light – I'd creep down the stairs to delight in the oranges and nuts he filled them with and a box of homemade candy a neighbor always sent us.

One day near Christmas I found a sprig of greenery on the sidewalk. I picked it up, coaxed Libby to give me her nickel allowance and with mine I bought three colorful balls in Woolworth's Five & Ten Cent Store. I decorated my itsy-bitsy branch and hid it in my closet. Weeks later my father happened to see it. All he said was, "Everyone else has thrown theirs away." He never scolded us, never spanked us, but my mother whacked me with a leather strap occasionally. When she wasn't looking one day I hid the strap under the center pedestal of our oak dining room table. She searched all over but never found it. I was never spanked again. Now I wonder how naughty I could have been. But rebellious I was at times.

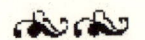

The Store

Again Memory rose and nudged me. I recalled Mama Casey about whom I hadn't thought in years. She was a neighbor in Greeneville. Her husband was a figure of authority, a policeman. At one time they lived across the street from us but then they moved a few blocks away up Central Avenue. On Saturday mornings when I was perhaps 10 years old I'd mosey up a few blocks to visit her in her new apartment. Why she tolerated me I don't know and why I was drawn to her I never asked myself. I liked her. She was pleasant, cheerful and someone different.

Of medium height, she was a small buxom figure covered in a large apron, black hair pinned to the top of her head, thick black brogans. Her warm, quick smile, her constant chatter with a brogue must have appealed to me. I enjoyed being in her bright kitchen as she merrily fussed and bustled about cooking and baking. I laugh as I remember the day she took a ham out of the oven and cut a snitch for me. I must have backed away. Ham was a forbidden food. But she persisted. "Eat it," she coaxed me. " 'Twon't do you no harm." I couldn't escape. I tasted it and liked it. It was good. I felt no remorse, no sense of sin. Nor did God come down from Heaven and smite me for my sin. "But don't you dare tell your father," she warned me. I never did.

Mama Casey had a beautiful daughter Loretta, tall, fair-haired and grown up. I admired her. Each Fourth of July she impersonated the Statue of Liberty. As the long parade crept down Central Avenue, my father, Libby and I crowded on the sidewalk, I would anxiously wait to see Loretta, crowned, arm uplifted, holding her lamp. I marveled at how she maintained her balance up in the air on the

I Remember Chesterfield

slowly moving float. Each time the American flag went by I glanced at my father who always placed his hand over his heart. How proud I felt of him. How happy I was that we were Americans.

My train of thought comes back to Chesterfield.

On one of our trips to my grandparents' farm, I remember a lovely summer day in July 1919 when I asked my father for permission to go down to Grandpa's store. After all, I was eight years old and entering fourth grade. When he relented and said, "Yes," I was out the door in a flash!

I dashed across the yard, scooted under the fence that separated it from the vegetable garden and crossed beneath the grape arbor where, in the heat, the hens were taking dust baths. Then, skimming down the hill on the narrow footpath running parallel to the road – the short cut we called it – I was almost hidden by the tall grasses brushing my shoulders. White daisies and the black-eyed Susan's I often wove in long chains, stately Queen Anne's lace, purple and white clover, unforgettable meadow fragrances. In a few moments I hopped across the teeny brook that seeped out of the swamp at the bottom of the hill and bounded into the musty dimness of the rear storeroom.

Motes of dust floated in the ray of pale sunshine streaming from a lone window high up. Against one wall burlap bags of grain were stacked. On the other wall rakes and scythes, pitchforks and shovels, pails and axes in neat order I barely glanced at. I didn't linger.

The Store

Quickly I opened the door and stepped up into the store. What treasures! What goodies!

On a high shelf Aunt Helen kept farmers' summer clothing: plaid shirts, blue and red neckerchiefs, visored caps, bib overalls with metal buckles, white work gloves and rubber boots. On a lower shelf canned goods were prominent. They were a luxury in those days. On the counter sat a huge red coffee grinder with big wheels, too heavy for me to turn. And, from the hook in the ceiling above hung a hand of bananas. Several dozen bananas clustered on a single stem was called "a hand." Below the counter open bags of sugar, dried beans, chick feed, sold by the pound, were displayed.

On the opposite wall an elevated, four-leg, glass container held 5 cent bottles of soda water with flavors such as sarsaparilla, root beer, lemon-lime, orange, strawberry, cream and vanilla, neck deep in water cooled by a hunk of ice my grandfather had cut last winter. Above this, a menacing poster of Bull Durham chew tobacco (some men rolled their own), packaged cigarettes, playing cards, writing supplies, shoe laces and sundries were for sale. But, best of all, the penny candy case held my heart. Neither Aunt Helen nor my grandfather ever remarked on how much candy I helped myself to. I chose my favorites from small square glass dishes in which she had painstakingly arranged chocolate sugar babies, miniature bolsters, Necco wafers of all colors (I culled the chocolate ones), petite chocolate covered mints, jaw breakers, licorice strings, red and black, lemon drops, peanut candy, sugar daddys, lollypops, all day suckers, non pareils, chewing gum. Aunt Helen, whose mortal enemies were dust and dirt, was forever polishing the fingerprints off that case. After eating my share of the 25 varieties or so, I sauntered outside onto the

I Remember Chesterfield

open roofed porch where my grandfather sat on a bench. I sat down next to him.

"Micala," he affectionately called me by my Jewish name, and began to tell me the latest episode of the story that ran in serial form in the daily Jewish newspaper *The Forward*, mailed from New York. He was enamored of the never-ending crises in the people's lives, the vagaries of their existence, the heart-rending drama and the diverse traits of the many characters. He mulled over their twists of fate.

Isi, one year old, 1910

Isadore Savin and his dog Aristotle, c. 1921

The Store

I listened, but not too intently. Soon Aunt Helen came and poked her head out the door. She looked up and down the road. "Here comes that wild Indian Isi Savin," she said. I watched him come barreling down the highway, pedaling so fast his dog Aristotle had trouble keeping pace. Throwing his bike against the porch, he leaped off before the wheels stopped spinning. Marching onto the store, he grabbed a banana announcing, "God helps those who help themselves," and was gone. Serious me, I thought he was so terrible, so blasphemous, I never forgot the incident.

Aunt Helen merely shrugged. "His mother has a charge account," she informed me. "He can have anything he wants."

I have a picture of him taken that summer. He's ten years old, a shock of short black hair, bright black eyes, faded bib overalls, hugging Aristotle and bursting with the energy he never lost, the same energy, restlessness and drive that enriched our 40 years of marriage and brought us many happy hours together.

As I write about this little episode that occurred when I was eight years old, I realize that this was the first time Aunt Helen became a definite character in the drama of my Chesterfield experience. Because she was the youngest daughter and utterly devoted to her parents and their welfare she stayed close to them all her life. Consequently, I saw more of Aunt Helen than I did of any other person in Chesterfield.

I Remember Chesterfield

Her older sisters had dark hair, dark eyes and resembled their parents. Aunt Helen's features were more angular, her skin unblemished and smooth as cream, her light brown hair held tapering touches of blonde. Although I never saw her do this, she must have secretly used a little peroxide, all of which made her very attractive. In an era when women pinched their cheeks and bit their lips for color Aunt Helen was daring. I admired her spunk and bit of naughtiness.

Whenever I saw Aunt Helen in Chesterfield she always wore plain serviceable clothes. But I remember when she was young and we shared the same attic bedroom, I would lie in bed and watch her dress. Meticulous she was. It took her quite a while to patiently secure her fine hair into a perfect low bun with at least 50 tiny wire hairpins. Occasionally when she visited her married sisters Molly and Rose in New York she would return with stunning clothes which she seldom wore in Chesterfield. I have a single vision of her as she stood in front of her small mirror assessing herself. She looked lovely in a slim vivid orange silk dress with a Peter Pan collar of gold metallic cloth material. She had a date that night.

From my observation Aunt Helen had little fun in her life. She always worked hard from the time she attended Chesterfield's one room schoolhouse. In a picture from that era I note how huge were the scalloped hair ribbons she wore stiffly on top of her light brown hair. After graduation she tended store with Grandpa and finally assumed the whole operation. I never heard her mention a movie, a dance, a concert, a Broadway show, seldom even a party. Nor did

The Store

Ida Kaplan holding Micki, Aunts Mollie and Goldie, unknown man, 1911

she ever comment about some fellow she met. She was not anxious to marry. She was fussy and there were few eligible men in the area.

However, in 1930 she did exchange wedding vows with a very nice man, Samuel May, who came from New York. They lived in the apartment over the store. The old store I remember from my childhood had burned down. This new one was similar but more spacious and the upstairs apartment was convenient.

As far back as I can remember Aunt Helen was always cleaning, dusting, polishing, arranging, wiping, cooking, puttering around. She waited on customers, chatting amiably, pumped gas, cared for her home, husband and children, Barbara and Ira. Nights when she had accomplished as many of her daily duties as she could she sat down to do her books. Customers had charge accounts and she kept detailed records.

"But I find myself falling asleep," she often complained to me.

Aunt Helen and I were never intimate friends. We didn't confess our hopes and dreams to each other. Though we had some common concerns and our children were of comparable ages, we did live different lives.

I visited her often. Whenever I passed through Chesterfield to and fro from the beach or if I happened to be on my way to New London, I usually stopped at the store to say "Hello." Some Sunday afternoons I would leave the Savin family gatherings to drive down to the village. Aunt Helen was always glad to see me.

She was particularly fond of Isi and he of her. Their relationship was of long standing. During the summer she would ask him whenever he traveled from Hartford to bring her fresh produce. I

The Store

remember he supplied her with baskets of ripe tomatoes, early apples, cucumbers and such to sell in the store.

Aunt Helen played another important role in the family. Though marooned in Chesterfield, she became the kingpin in her extended family. She maintained constant touch with those dear to her. My loving, warm, maternal Aunt Rose was often impoverished because in the early 20th century people like her husband, who worked in the needle industry, were laid off between seasons. Aunt Helen mailed her money and food packages. She cared for Rose's children, especially Violet, and for Aunt Molly's daughter Elaine about whose beauty she raved. To all Aunt Helen was kind, generous, gracious, always giving everyone gifts which I felt she really couldn't afford. I would never refuse her largesse. She'd be hurt.

She played another role, a genuine center of information. Often people who had summered in Chesterfield, or members of their families, would visit the area to reminisce or discover some relic and would naturally seek out Aunt Helen. She always welcomed them and helped when she could.

Over the years I watched Aunt Helen grow old. Her body bent over and she shuffled in her walk. Her hair deepened in color and she wore it plain, cut to below ear length. Times in Chesterfield were not prosperous for her. The population diminished. The era of summer folk was long gone and the few local shoppers found it easier to drive to New London supermarkets for needy purchases.

The ills of aging did not exclude Aunt Helen. The two dramatic, monumental experiences in her later life that opened new horizons for her were the medical evaluation she received in Boston, she talked about this often, and the stay in the convalescent home in

I Remember Chesterfield

New London after her heart attack. But she retained her spirit, her doggedness, her determination and her genuine interest in people. (Aunt Helen is pictured on page 72.)

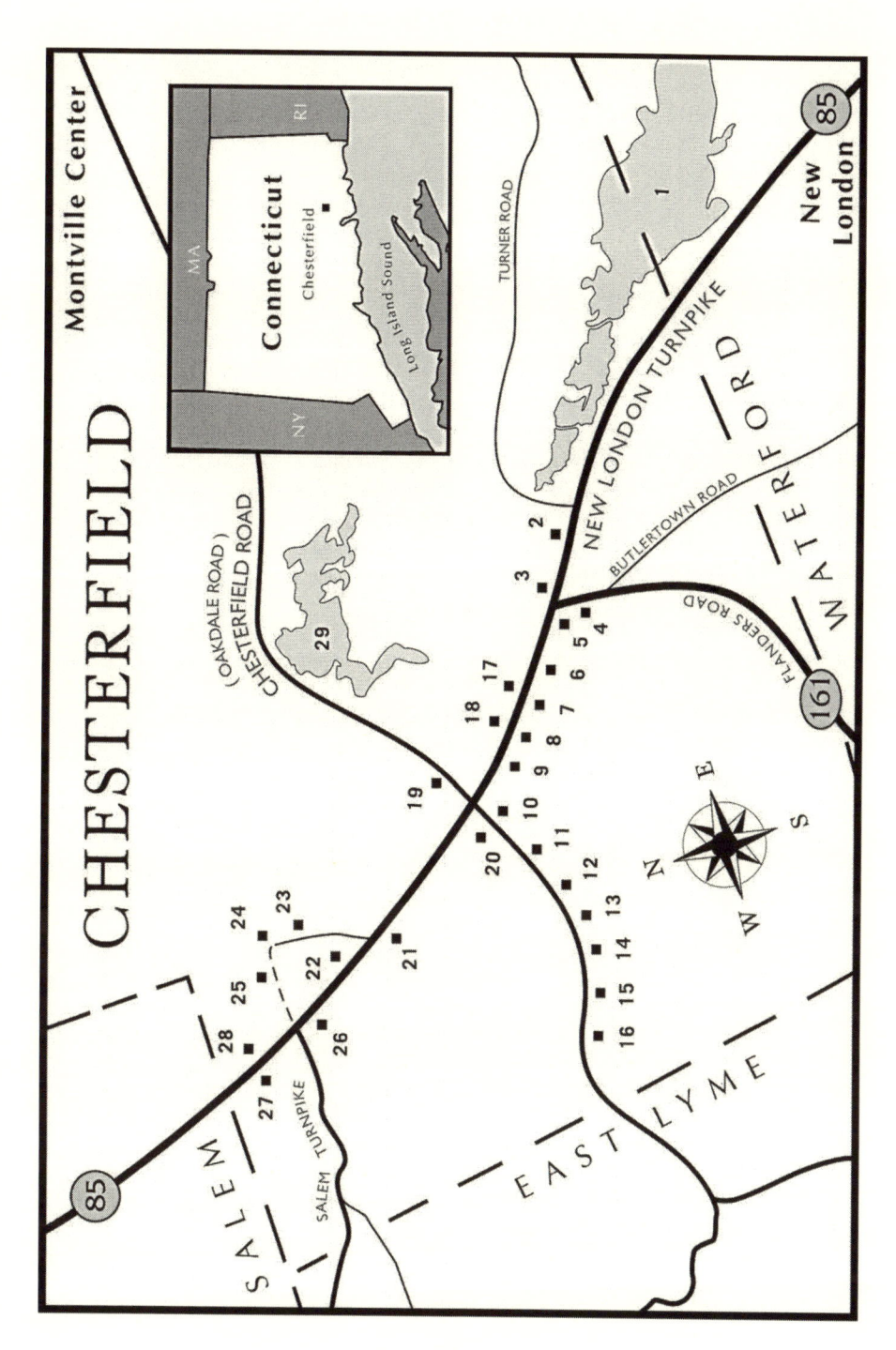

The Store

I Remember Chesterfield

MAP OF CHESTERFIELD

1. Lake Konomoc Reservoir
2. Issac Kaplan farm
3. Power's house
4. Miller's house
5. Synagogue
6. Grandpa's dance hall
7. Grandpa's general store
8. Mr. Miller's butcher shop
9. Small dwelling
10. Jake and Doris Kaplan's house
11. Grandpa and Grandma's farm
12. Tinker homestead
13. Greenberg's summer home
14. Grodinsky's summer home
15. Anapolsky's summer home
16. Leviloff farm
17. Dwelling opposite Grandpa's store
18. Yardofski's store
19. Abandoned Jewish cemetery on Chapel Hill
20. One-room schoolhouse
21. Kosofski's brook and house
22. Schwartz farm
23. Bond's brook
24. Bond homestead
25. Mrs. Savin's little house
26. Mrs. Savin's big house
27. Cohen farm
28. Mrs. Wickson's house
29. Boque Brook Reservoir

This map of Chesterfield, as remembered by the author and created by Yohanna S. Willheim, is based on a map of the western half of Montville and has been used with the permission of Harbor Publications, Inc., Madison, Connecticut.

Chesterfield As I First Knew It
Chapter VII

I must have been 11 or 12 years old when the physical entity, Chesterfield, found its focus in my intelligence. Up until then Chesterfield meant only my Grandparents' farm and general store. Now I became acquainted with most of the places and some of the people who inhabited this limited area all the way from the farm of Uncle Isaac, Grandpa's brother, that crested the long hill on the highway emanating from New London to the properties of Mrs. Savin, my future mother-in-law, as they met the Salem line.

Chesterfield had no library, no picturesque village green, no Police Station. Occasionally a Connecticut State Trooper would stop at Grandpa's store and chat with Aunt Helen and whoever was around. Chesterfield had no Town Hall. As I noted before, all legal transactions and vital statistics were entered in the annals of Montville. Mail came addressed to RFD Chesterfield, Oakdale, Connecticut, about 7 miles away. I remember the pleasant, weather-beaten face of the mailman. I think his name was Harry. The black car he drove, probably a Ford, had a top but no windows. To the residents he sold stamps, delivered their packages and letters and carried away their outgoing mail. The mailman's arrival was eagerly awaited each day. And I remember I was surprised Harry never gossiped.

On the northwest corner of the highway, bisected by the Oakdale Road, stood the one room schoolhouse which my mother and her siblings attended, as well as the next generation including Isi,

I Remember Chesterfield

my husband. Here Chesterfield children received their basic elementary education. For further study boys went to Buckley High School, girls to Williams Memorial, both in New London.

Clustered at the bottom of the long hill, in a segment of the road no more than 300 feet, was a group of small houses and stores, individually owned, Grandpa's store prominent among them. This was the only close arrangement of buildings in Chesterfield and we called this The Village. The store with its spacious, uncluttered interior and open porch had become a gathering place, a center of activity. Local men, gents, liked to meet there and "chew the fat". In the summer the place was exceedingly popular. For the lack of anything more interesting to do, summer guests at the several farms would saunter or drive down on a gentle summer evening to the store. They would greet friends, mill around, buy a snack and talk, creating an ambience of camaraderie, an intimate, impromptu affair, night after night. Grandpa's store was certainly the place to be.

Adjoining the store on one side was Mr. Miller's small, neat butcher shop. He was a short, serious, wizened man. Isi had a favorite story about Mr. Miller. It always makes me laugh as I recount it because I can so easily picture the scene as Isi described it:

> Old man Miller had a horse named Nellie. Smart horse she was. Every afternoon when Miller made his meat deliveries to the different farms, he would doze off. He didn't worry. Nellie knew the way and all the stops. But then, Miller decided to go modern. He bought himself a small Ford car. Well, Pat Tinker and I were sitting outside on the bench at your grandfather's store that day. Just talking. I happened to look up and there, at the top of the hill, I saw Miller's car. He had lost control. Down it came, a mile a

minute! As he whipped by us I could see him, half out of his seat, madly clutching the wheel, flopping up and down and he's yelling 'Whoa, Nellie. Whoa, whoa, Whooaa!' Pat and I laughed so hard. We just cracked up.

On the other side of the store was a low, white structure, Grandpa's Dance Hall. People came from all around the area each Wednesday and Saturday night to dance to the music of Wesley Hanney and his Orchestra. The one-step, a lively two-step, fox trot, a vigorous polka, an occasional waltz and several country square dances. "Dig for the Oyster, Shuck for the Clam," "Turkey in The Straw, Wish't I Had a Mother-in-law," "… Circle your lady …" the caller would sing out, … "and Promenade." Wonderful nights of pure joy. But not for me. I was too young and too shy to join the crowd. Nor would my father approve of me dancing with a stranger. By the time I was old enough the Dance Hall no longer existed.

The Miller family, whom my cousin Violet, Aunt Rose's daughter, and I enjoyed visiting, had a house at the junction of the Flanders Road and the highway, which had been the Creamery Baron de Hirsch built and was now converted. Violet and I were friendly with the three younger daughters, Fanny, Sylvia and Lily. Mrs. Miller, a homespun, hospitable person, always greeted us with a big smile and offered us a lavish array of delicious desserts. Especially at Passover which to me is a contest to discover how many different dishes can be dreamed up out of eggs and matzo. I remember Bessie, the eldest daughter, who made a scrumptious, light as a feather, gorgeous sponge cake. I still retain her recipe:

1. Beat 12 egg yolks with the juice of a lemon and 1/2 cup of sugar until light yellow.
2. Fold in slowly 12 egg whites beaten with 1 cup of sugar.
3. Fold in 1 cup of sifted Passover cake meal, 1/2 cup of potato starch and the grated rind of a lemon.
4. Bake at 350 degrees for one hour.

Now I wonder how long it took her to do this without an electric mixer.

I never met any of the Powers family who lived opposite the Millers and in whose small front yard pond neighbors cut ice in the winter. Nor did I ever see Willie Yardusky whose rival store was diagonally across the highway from Grandpa's. I knew only one elderly couple, the Leviloffs, who occupied one of the four little houses in The Village. I could recognize the Schwartz and Cohen homes up the road and I often met and conversed with Pat Tinker, a tall, fair, amiable Yankee gentleman, who maintained his family's homestead just beyond Grandpa's farm. And beyond his place, in the late 1920's three New York families built summer homes, the Greenbergs, Anapolskys and Grodinskis. The Kosofskis also had a summer home. Two other families, Zaist and Muzurkowitz, I merely heard of. In fact, even then, there weren't that many people left in Chesterfield. Only the elderly farmers remained and no longer farmed. Except for Aunt Helen and Uncle Jake, most of their children, healthy, strong and ambitious, had sought their fortunes elsewhere.

Of course, over the years changes occurred in Chesterfield but nothing basic seemed to disturb the rural harmony. This feeling of peace and quiet and nature's rhythm is something I loved all my life.

As I write this chapter I am reminded of my Freshman class at Connecticut College where in my fifth year of studying Latin, our professor, Dean Nye, assigned for translation several pastoral poems composed by Horace, one of ancient Rome's noted poets. In them he longs for, praises and envies the tranquil life of the farmer. I do know that farmers have problems, even those 2000 years ago, and labor long hours. Yet I have always retained an admiration for the simplicity and dependability of my Grandparents' lives, the regularity of their daily routine, the peace and beauty of the land, their acceptance of Nature's challenges and the satisfaction they must have felt at the end of a day's work well done. No matter where I lived in my life or went, the love for nature, grass, trees, open sky, wind, hot sun, sweet scented air ... all that I early experienced in Chesterfield ... has stayed with me and influenced my life.

I Remember Chesterfield

The Kaplan family at my grandparents' homestead

The Kaplan family, c. 1930. Top row: (l - r) Joe Rudy, Molly, Ida, Sam May, Helen, Fred Herman, Goldie, Louis Saul, Rose. Middle Row: Ruth Solomon, Burton Rudy, Elaine Meisner, Bernard Saul. Bottom row: Alfred Meisner and Grandma Sarah, holding Barbara May.

The Farm
Chapter VIII

A small, irregular plateau about 500 feet in diameter crowned a short stubby hill and enclosed my grandparents' farmhouse, shabby outbuildings, garden and orchard. The driveway thrust sharply upward from the single lane dirt road, circled the house and fell back in a long slant to the lane, deeply rutted and in the spring thick with mud. The house faced the top of the driveway. Its seldom-used front door with two slender, pretty glass panels opened into a somber, dark hall. How well I remember the deep, unlit alcove at its far end. Here were the stairs to the second floor. Here, every morning, before we had electricity about 1930, Aunt Helen vigorously polished last night's sooted glass chimneys from the many kerosene lamps.

At the right of the hall were two rooms back to back: the quiet parlor, shadowed by the outside porch and tall shrubs, nicely furnished but never used in my time, and my grandparents' bedroom open to the kitchen. Their high bed, built against the wall, was tucked under the window and needed a stepstool to get into it. On the left side of the hall were two similar rooms, a bit smaller and used as bedrooms.

In back of these four rooms and hall and across most of the width of the house stretched the cozy, ample kitchen. I remember the shiny blue and white linoleum squares on the floor, the stiff black horsehair sofa over which hung a Currier and Ives print. On the opposite wall stood the black wood-burning stove, its nickel trim polished, and its wood box. Between two large windows that looked out across the driveway to the orchard a large square table was placed. On a shelf above this a kitchen clock ticked away the hours. Six doors opened off the kitchen, to the hall, the bedroom, outside porch, bathroom, two small rooms, probably "borning rooms" that Grandma used for storage, and the little sink room. Close to the outside door a wall telephone, a party line servicing six or more families, gave Grandma the opportunity of listening in on the conversations.

The teeny sink room, distinguished by its large black iron sink and cold water hand pump, connected the kitchen to the summer dining room and the outside back door. On a low shelf opposite the sink two large shiny metal buckets were kept filled with good, pure well water. I loved to dip a tin cup, it had to be tin, on a hot summer day into the water's coolness. I'd wait for the beads of moisture to form on the cup, then drink greedily. I can still remember that delicious, wonderfully refreshing taste.

The spacious rectangular summer dining room was designed with three large uncurtained windows on opposite walls. Under them and along each wall was placed a full length table with long benches on each side. They could seat 50 – 60 people who ate facing each other. Nothing adorned the plain walls of slender matchboard painted white. In the corner near the outside door stood a square, flat top, old-fashioned black mahogany piano with four heavy legs. Its broken keys made strange sounds, tinny sounds when I tried to play it. Obviously the piano was a relic of the days of the boarders when each evening they created their own entertainment. Grandpa had never bothered to throw the old piano away.

The Farm

The barebones summer kitchen, a lean-to wooden structure as wide as the dining room, had no doors so the air could circulate better. I remember the brown wooden icebox. Into the tin lined compartment at the top Grandpa placed a block of ice. As it melted, water dripped into a flat pan underneath. We monitored it carefully lest it overflow onto the wood floor. Later on, because the summer kitchen had no extra space, a commodious electric refrigerator was placed close by in the dining room. Three tiers of long shelves to hold food supplies and crockery hung on one wall. Corresponding with the shelves was a long worktable. A wood burning stove and an iron sink with a cold water pump filled the room. I smile as I recollect the many times I'd walk into this summer kitchen in the late afternoon for something to eat. I'd see, perhaps, the crisp browned chicken in Grandma's blue enamel roasting pan, a blueberry pie, a loaf of her fragrant, mouth-watering bread, freshly baked, all pushed to the side of the stove. She never scolded if I snitched the wing of the chicken or cut into the pie or slobbered blueberry jam on a slice of bread.

THE OUTBUILDINGS

Several outbuildings edged part of the perimeter of the plateau. Beyond the summer kitchen and across the driveway stood an open shed with a roof, the Wash House. On two benches across from each other were assembled six or eight galvanized wash tubs, corrugated wash boards, bars of Fels Naptha soap and a few copper boilers. A large black wood-burning stove and a stack of wood were situated between the benches. On Monday mornings Grandpa would fill two huge barrels of water drawn from the spring somewhere on his land and with a horse and travois bring them close to the Wash House. Then the women, including summer guests, would spend the morning washing their laundry. After the clothes had been scrubbed, rinsed, wrung and boiled they were strung on sagging lines or spread on the grass where the sun bleached them. At night I thought it felt heavenly to sleep between the pure white sheets smelling so sweet and clean. When the women needed to iron anything they heated the old fashioned flat irons on the stove, then clamped on a wooden handle. To test the proper temperature my mother used to spit on her iron and note how it sizzled.

The Ice House was further along, a heavy weather worn door opened into a small wooden building where stacked blocks of ice were insulated in layers of saw dust. When I was a child I'd like to sneak into the cool darkness if Grandpa was there. It was cozy and mysterious. He'd chip off a piece of ice and clean it for me. I'd lick its delicious coolness but I had to be very careful not to let it drip on my dress. My mother surely wouldn't like that.

It was in front of these two buildings that the *shoket* (butcher) would come on Thursday mornings to kill, according to ritual law, the chickens for the Sabbath dinner. Once he had cut the vein in the neck, the chicken would stagger around for a while before toppling over. I was fascinated by this. If the chicken were supposedly dead how could it still be walking? And I remember my mother! How she detested hand plucking those chicken feathers, especially the tiny black ones so deeply imbedded and difficult to pull out. I remember how explicitly and often she stated her displeasure. To ease the task, singeing over an open fire was allowed, but Jewish law did not permit scalding with hot water to relax the pores.

The Farm

A space away, a large barn held the wagon and buggy on the ground floor. In the loft above, hay for winter fodder was stored. Riding the hay wagon when I was a child was the most fun. When Grandpa and Uncle Jake were cutting hay with scythes, we kids, Libby, my four cousins and I, would gather in the meadow to watch. When the wagon was piled high enough, Uncle Jake would toss each one of us onto the top and we'd ride all the way to the barn, giggling and thrilled, the hay prickling our backsides as we jolted along.

The cow and horse barn was off a ways under the rim of the plateau. I seldom went to this barn. This was not my territory except for one treat. If we happened to stay overnight on the farm I'd wake early, slip on my robe, shoes, take a big white cup from the summer kitchen and mosey down in the fragrant, cool morning to the barn where Uncle Jake was milking. I'd hang around near the door where the cats waited patiently for a handout. I didn't dare to get close to the big animals contentedly chewing, their tails slapping left and right at the flies. I was afraid of them. I didn't want one to lash out suddenly and kick me. Uncle Jake would take my cup and fill it with warm milk. Unpasteurized, not skimmed, it was delicious.

But the word "barn" flushed another scene out of my Memory.

༺༻

I recall the spring of 1966 when Isi and I were motoring through the Chateau country of France. We always traveled by ourselves, free to choose our own itinerary, free to change on a whim. Isi liked to drive. "I can better remember what I see," he'd say.

I Remember Chesterfield

He preferred to drive the French automobile Citroen. "It's so homely," he'd laugh, "it's beautiful."

New roads, strange roads, roads obviously not often used appealed to him. "Let's see where they go," he'd tell me. One afternoon we were riding crosslots. Country roads, not identified, crisscrossed, forked, zigzagged, met, merged and fascinated him. We passed miles of verdant growth, fields of blooming rap, acres of yellow mustard flowers and stands of golden gorse along the roadsides. Rural France was gorgeous that day. Blue sky and fertile fields rich in yellow and green. I spied a wee sign, Chateau Villesavin. We detoured and discovered a charming small chateau. We enjoyed walking around it.

Then Isi chose a little road that became narrower and narrower and ended abruptly in a farmer's barnyard. He slammed on the brakes. The hens ran squawking, the frightened ducks quacked madly, the geese scattered and the farmer's young wife came running.

"We've come 3,000 miles," I muttered, "and you land up in a barnyard just like Chesterfield, manure pile and all."

I stepped out of the car and in my meager French asked her how to get back to the main road. She was kind. With many gestures and some words I recognized she sent us on our way. When we could, we stopped and had a good laugh. What did she think of two foolish Americans who blundered into her barnyard?

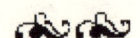

The Farm

    As it completed its circumference, the plateau of Grandpa's land accommodated an apple orchard where several hammocks were strung between the gnarled trees. On an afternoon when there was nothing left to do, how delightful it was to laze in one of the hammocks and rock in the shade as I waited for supper. Mother and Aunt Rose never asked us to help in the kitchen. Grandpa didn't fuss with the orchard so we kids could take whatever apples we wanted. No one climbed the trees. We waited for the fruit to drop. There was only one Golden Delicious apple tree that ripened early in August. It was my favorite. How truly delicious that first, small, sun ripened apple tasted.

    One of my humorous memories about the orchard goes back to one summer night so hot it was impossible to sleep inside the house. Not a breath of air stirred. Not a leaf fluttered. The accumulated heat in the house made the bedrooms impossible to sleep. So everyone, summer renters included, even friends who drove out from Norwich for relief, dragged mattresses and pillows from the house and spread them in the orchard. We all slept outside. I thought everybody looked so funny in their nightclothes.

    Across the rear of the orchard and all the way down to the barn Grandpa and Uncle Jake had strung a barbed wire fence. Now the cows, meandering up from the meadows on their way to the evening milking, could not make a dash for the fruit on the ground. But we kids could easily bend under the lowest barrier, scoot down the hill, hop the brook, skirt the swamp and wander into the sunny meadows.

    In this small area, the plateau, the center of my Chesterfield existence when I was young, I spent countless happy hours of fun,

I Remember Chesterfield

play and adventure. Responsibilities of the farm were not given to us children. I remember every day was like a jewel. We children never fought among ourselves. We girls just played the summer days away, playing house, imitating our mothers. We spent hours weaving long chains of daisies and decorating ourselves. We played tag in the orchard and on the steps of the house bounced our balls and jacks. The boys trailed my Grandfather and Uncle Jake and got into plenty of mischief. I don't remember anyone being punished.

The Accident
Chapter IX

Midwinter, January 1925. We did not visit my grandparents in Chesterfield for a while. The car had no heater and the snow-covered roads would be too difficult to navigate.

We were happy that winter living in the beautiful new home my parents had built the previous June at 234 Broadway in Norwich, only a few blocks from the Academy where I was a freshman. I loved the house, so bright and airy. The wide sweep of the front porch, the large living room where my mother had draped a handsome embroidered silk Spanish shawl over my piano. In the spacious dining room stood the elegant, well polished, Jacobean furniture my mother had taken me to New York to help her select. Though I was only 12-years-old, I presume she didn't want to go alone, and then my mother always asked and trusted my opinions. Off the kitchen, long before a family room or a den was introduced, we had a room where I did my homework. The laundry was on the first floor and in the basement a coal furnace provided indoor heating, an innovation at the time. Upstairs there were four cheerful bedrooms and a glassed-in sun parlor. When I lay in my bedroom near the front window I could watch, fascinated, the treetop sway in the wind. And my mother, who was an excellent housekeeper and fabulous ironer, now had a maid.

In my memory I hold a picture, shadowy and indistinct, of my father on that deep, nebulous gray, overcast afternoon, January 20, his body a blur in the high-backed chair near the unlit fireplace, the

I Remember Chesterfield

window behind him a dull black square. Home from school, I had walked into the living room, probably to practice at the piano. I was surprised to find him sitting quietly in the silent gloom. I thought it was strange. What was he doing home so early? Later on I wondered if he had had a vague premonition of the imminent tragedy. Did he suspect some dire omen? When he saw me he began to talk seriously. I couldn't understand why.

I was only 13 years old, on the threshold of young womanhood, my whole life ahead of me, secure. So why was my Victorian father, steeped in the high morals of traditional Judaism, concerned that day about how I would grow up, how I should comport myself in the future, to always remember to be a proper lady in every respect and, as the oldest child, I would be responsible? (As he was.) What's he talking about I thought? I shrugged off his words.

A week later he was gone.

But the context of the message he implied has long lingered with me. Despite sorrow and dismay I did not seek refuge in sex, alcohol or drugs. All my life, sometimes not so successfully, I did endeavor to meet his expectations. I remember my psychiatrist years later telling me, "You tried to wear your father's shoes." He was right. My mother gave me freedom too. She trusted me. With no role model to follow I pioneered. I early learned that if I wanted something I had to find the way myself. It turned out to be a valuable lesson.

I can never forget the night of my father's accident. Snow and ice covered the frozen earth on Friday, January 23, 1925. A bitter cold, pitch black afternoon. I was alone in the house. My mother, her sister Helen and my sisters had not returned from shopping. Nor was my father home yet. I was upstairs in my room – so excited, just like

The Accident

everyone else in the area. For tomorrow, the following morning, Saturday, a phenomenon, a total eclipse of the sun, was going to plunge Eastern Connecticut into an awe-inspiring, spectacular darkness. In my lifetime this would never again happen in Norwich. My father had bought Libby and me smoked glasses so we could trace the ominous shadow of the moon creep across the winter sun, blotting out the familiar light, the fiery corona blazing in the blackened sky, proving the mystery of the heavens and striking fear and wonder in our hearts.

I remember the telephone rang about 5:30 that Friday afternoon. I ran downstairs to answer it.

A voice asked, "Is this the home of Morris Solomon?"

"Yes."

"I'm calling from the Backus Hospital. There's been an accident. Mr. Solomon has been brought here. He is seriously injured."

I don't remember the rest of the conversation. Later I learned the story.

When my father, who was still at the grain store in Greeneville, discovered that a customer in Moosup, about 20 miles north of Norwich, had not received his weekend order, he decided to deliver it himself. The roads were icy, the driving treacherous. After giving the merchant his supplies, my father started for home. He had to cross the railroad tracks that ran through the center of Moosup. There was no signalman to warn him. By the time he noticed the flashing lights signifying an approaching train it was too late. He stepped on the brakes. The car skidded onto the open tracks. The

I Remember Chesterfield

unscheduled train, coming from Boston filled with people eager to witness the eclipse, smashed into him.

The next two days were a nightmare. I was told he never regained consciousness. My mother did not take me to see him.

On Monday morning his body came home and lay on the living room floor. There were no Jewish funeral parlors at that time to soften the heartrending problems. I clearly remember how I stood by myself in the front hall, watching the steady stream of mourners circling the room, softly weeping.

He was buried that afternoon, January 26, 1925.

Thus ended my childhood.

My mother collapsed and went to bed for a month. All was chaos.

My father was only 45 years old. Emigrating to America 25 years ago, he worked hard and prospered. He was highly thought of, well respected, but he left no will, dying intestate. There was considerable money in his estate however, and a double indemnity insurance policy as well as the shares he owned in a Corporation he had formed after World War I with two other grain companies in the area.

The Solomon family, also devastated by the tragic death of their leader, their protector, their beloved brother, asked my mother to turn over $10,000 as a dowry for the unmarried sister Toby. This request did not endear them to my mother. She refused. She needed everything to care for and educate her children. My sister Ruth was only 4 years old.

Then they suggested to her that she entrust the money to Morris's Uncle Michael Levin who was married to Morris's mother's sister, Aunt Annie. He was a prosperous, wealthy man, who knew about financial matters. With no kind of understanding how to best utilize the inheritance, my mother did that. Uncle became administrator of Morris's estate, answerable to Probate Court. When she finally realized that she had to submit a request to Michael Levin for the money she needed, she was furious. She had lost control.

To add to the problems, the Corporation my father belonged to offered her a meager amount for my father's share of stock. They would accept no other arrangement. They wanted to buy her out. And when she learned that they had sold the same shares to Michael Levin's son for $35,000 more than they paid her, she really hit the ceiling. She raved and ranted and carried on. Which was difficult for me. I loved my father's family and felt loyal to them too.

In time, of course, my mother quieted down and adjusted to her tragedy and misfortune. She learned to drive. Now we spent much more time in Chesterfield, weekends and parts of summer vacations.

My father had no sons to recite the *Kaddish,* the mourners' Hebrew prayer praising God. Twice a day, at morning and evening services, sons go to synagogue for one year. The *Kaddish* is also recited on the anniversary of death. My mother hired someone to pay my father this honor. Yet, somehow I felt the need to go too. So Libby and I, whenever we were in Chesterfield on Saturday mornings, walked to the little *shul.* In front of the Ark we two girls stood and joined the others in the *Yis-ga-dal, v'yis-ka-dash sh'may rabo.* Blessed be the name of the Lord.

I don't know if the elderly gentlemen worshippers approved of us girls doing this, but nobody stopped us or criticized us. Their

I Remember Chesterfield

hearts must have ached too at the tremendous loss of a man too young to die, so special a human being, a friend to all, and loving his life. And for us who now had to grow up without the comfort and guidance of a precious and doting father.

Halcyon Days in Chesterfield
Chapter X

I often think back to the time after my father's death when, during parts of the summers of 1925-26, being in Chesterfield opened new vistas for me. My mother felt more comfortable there and we spent long stretches of time with my grandparents. I delighted in the open spaces, the uninterrupted span of wide sky, nature's sheer beauty, the absence of turmoil. I found comfort in the basic simplicity of living, the accepted rhythm of daily life and, of course, in the tacit love of my grandparents, I remember how often I'd daydream of someday possessing a "gentlelady's" farm with hired help to run it.

Yet, despite my enjoyment, in the very pit of my stomach lay an ache, a restless malaise I couldn't identify, I couldn't voice. In my heart I still mourned my father, the one person I could trust and who loved me unequivocally. I missed his family, but my mother was estranged from them. She felt they had betrayed her. There were several paternal cousins close to whom I longed to be, to share their jokes, their intimacy, our common background. But I was an unwilling outsider. And the Solomon family made no effort to contact my sisters or me. They stayed away.

Nor was I really an intrinsic part of the Chesterfield community. Not living there year round, not going to school with the other students, not participating in their day-to-day routine, I was not rooted in Chesterfield. I was studying Greek and Latin, Ancient History and English. I didn't know what they studied in their schools.

I Remember Chesterfield

Then too, I felt somewhat shunned. I was not "bee aye you ti ful" as Aunt Helen pronounced it. My mother told me I wasn't pretty and who should know better than she? To her family beauty was a major criterion. Violet, Aunt Rosie's daughter, born 6 months before me, seemed to be the favored first grandchild. She was more aggressive than I and more realistic.

And everyone fussed over my younger sister, Libby, the acquiescent goody girl and "cute as a button." After my father died someone asked her what she would like. "A doll," she answered. I never played with dolls. Libby was far less demanding than I and she was not mature enough to be a companion. We never discussed our problems together. I felt pretty much alone.

There was no one else to whom I could confess my disquiet which I tried to ignore. Yet I cherished everything Chesterfield offered me from Aunt Rose's delicious custards, which my mother never made, to the indolence of summer.

Upstairs in the old gray weather-beaten farmhouse were five bedrooms, but I preferred to sleep in the single finished bedroom in the attic. Aunt Helen slept in one double bed, I in the other.

If the morning happened to be a softly raining one I'd lie snug in the dampness listening to the irregular patter on the uninsulated roof. Pit, pat, pit a pat, pit, pit ... "rain before 7, clear before 11." Or, if it were a soft, dewy morning, a gentle cool breeze would rise, stir the white ruffled curtains at the open screened windows, fragrant smells, redolent of summer, drifting through the room. If the day promised to be bright and pleasant I'd dress and go down to breakfast where Grandma waited on me. She preferred to do this and anyhow, I wouldn't know how to handle the wood stove. Then, usually I'd like to go blueberrying. Occasionally Violet came along. We'd drape empty coffee cans, suspended by strings, around our necks, saunter across the orchard, scoot under the barbed wire fence, amble down the hill, hop the little brook, the same one that further on meandered past the rear of Grandpa's store, and enter the meadows.

I'd like to crush a few spicy smelling leaves of wintergreen or bayberry and carry them in my pocket. We'd mosey along skirting the dried turds, slowly picking the berries clustered like blue pearls on low sprays. So peaceful it was. Only the delicate tinkle of cowbells floated from a distant lot. As the sun rose overhead and the heat of the day increased we'd move into the woods. Here the berries, big and bright blue, grew on tall shrubs. And when we thought we had enough we'd head for home. Violet always knew the way out of the woods and as she walked she ate her berries. Not I. I saved mine for the pie Grandma would bake. Blueberry pie is still my choice dessert.

Some mornings I'd walk across the yard to the hen house to gather the freshly laid eggs and take them to Grandma. I'd be wary of the setting hens. If I approached one too close she'd ruffle her feathers, raise her sharp beak and prepare to attack me. Or, I'd like to wander in the vegetable garden, there was no flower garden, and pull out of the black earth fat carrots and deep red beets. On Monday mornings it was fun helping mother hang the wet laundry in the hot sun.

The big treat was afternoon swimming in Kosofski's brook, about a half-mile north on the main road.

The Kays, as the Kosofski family was familiarly called, were unusual in this simple working-farmer village of Chesterfield. Mr. Kay

I Remember Chesterfield

had made his fortune in the Alaska Gold Rush. Why he purchased their summer home in Chesterfield was a mystery to me and no one ever discussed it. The Kay's land abutted the Savin acres and Isi told me that when he was young the Kosofskis would come from New York with governesses and pony carts for their children.

The Kays were friendly whenever I met them, especially the parents. But they were a different cut of material. All of them were tall, slender, well built and distinguished looking in appearance, contrasting sharply to most of the Chesterfield Jewish people who were of medium height or short and stocky. They dressed differently too, more elegantly and sophisticated. We seldom saw them around. They did not mingle but stayed unto themselves. However, if the Jewish New Year holidays fell early in September, Mr. and Mrs. Kay would attend services at the little synagogue and contribute generously to the expenses.

In the lovely, clear brook which flowed between their house and the road the Kays graciously permitted anyone of the community to swim. From a shadowed upper meadow, where on both sides tall shrubs dipped their dark leaves in the transparent water, the brook came into view. It flowed over a deep hole into which the big boys jumped and splashed everyone around. Then, broadening out, it streamed over a sandy bed, so clear I could easily distinguish the tiny pebbles and grains of sand, and disappeared into high grasses. On the bank nearest the road the Kays had erected a large bathhouse, partitioned for separate sexes. I remember one day while I was changing my clothes Mrs. Kosofski began to undress. I noticed, surprising to my young eyes, how her stomach's stretched flesh hung in folds. Later I learned she had had 23 pregnancies, but only nine of her children grew to maturity.

No matter how hot the summer day, the brook water was cool and gentle. Sitting on a flat stone I'd take the soap I had brought and lather my long dark hair and body, submerging myself and let the soothing water wash over me. Turning over, it was an easy swim for me, maybe 15 feet, back up to the head of the open water where I'd flip over again and float back with the current. Sometimes my mother would pile all the children on the farm into the car and drive to Ocean Beach, about 10 miles away, but I always preferred Kay's brook, sweet, caressing, refreshing. Recently I met Alfred, one of the Kay grandchildren, who now lives in the summer home year round. He told me that the beautiful brook water was not the same. It had been diverted to the New London reservoir.

In the late afternoon whoever was swimming with me at Kay's brook and I would leisurely stroll home to the farm where we'd loll and relax until suppertime. It was a lulling time of the day. The sun slowly setting. The birds quiet, and a kind of hush lay over the land. There was always a sway in the hammock, a good book to read, a dawdling conversation to be had. Sometimes Violet and I would visit the Miller girls and Mrs. Miller's hospitality could spoil our appetites for supper. Her sweets were delicious.

In the evening I'd join the crowd gathering at Grandpa's store. The summer people there consisted mostly of New Yorkers who rented rooms with cooking privileges, although some farmers still hosted boarders. I remember with affection the Kushner family who came from Brooklyn for several summers. In 1928 Uncle Jake married Doris Kushner whom I liked very much. She was a down-to-

I Remember Chesterfield

earth person, outspoken and worldlier than anyone else I knew. When they lived in Chesterfield I visited them often.

How vividly I can recall an episode on a hot summer evening when I was 15. It was the end of a long hot, humid spell and as the sun set, storm clouds piled up on the horizon. Darkness approached; the air became electric. Exultant, I stood on the porch outside the kitchen door, alone. Night had fallen. For the past hour thunder had menacingly rumbled in the distance. Magnificent rivers of lightening slashed the heavens again and again. Silver streaks of blinding brilliance zigzagged and in an eye's wink vanished beyond the distant dim horizon. Nature was angry and I reveled in her fury. Inside the house our people cowered around the long dining room table, the pale light of kerosene lamps illuminating their tense faces. They talked in hushed whispers, struggling to minimize their fear. But I, defiant to fear, boldly watched the approaching storm. Suddenly, tumultuous winds blew up, whipping the stately trees along the dusty lane into twirling dervishes, torturing them into ghastly shapes. Then the rains came, pounding the parched foliage, flooding the hardened earth, drenching me with cool spray.

And I was glad. The heat wave was over.

As I write and think back to why this particular episode stayed with me so long, why I was so enraptured by the storm's violence, I can only believe that it echoed my own buried misgivings. And I learned I wasn't afraid. I wasn't afraid.

Chesterfield taught me that.

Halcyon Days in Chesterfield

Micki, Graduate of Norwich Free Academy, 1928

My Teens

Chapter XI

The halcyon days of Chesterfield ceased for me in May 1927 when my mother married Joseph Rudy. We moved from our lovely spacious home in Norwich to a much smaller, less attractive home at 72 Canterbury Street in Hartford, Connecticut, near Weaver High School. The ages of Joe's sons, Sidney, 12 and Burton 7, dovetailed with us girls. I was 16, Libby 14 and Ruth 6. For the next few summers all five of us were sent off to camps in Maine.

Ever since the past winter people had been trying to find a husband for my mother. She was 37 and widowed for 2 years, young, idealistic, romantic and rich. Me, I was terribly resentful. How could she marry anyone else? She spurned one suitor from New York and another from Boston. But Joe Rudy appealed to her and she married him after a brief acquaintance.

I remember the morning I walked into the Academy and my friends said to me, "I see your mother got married."

"How do you know?" ... I didn't.

"It's in this morning's paper."

I quickly found a copy of the *Norwich Bulletin* and there was the notice:

Ida Solomon and Joseph Rudy applied for a marriage license. She hadn't even told me!

I will say that Ida, as I liked to call her, took the same care of his two boys as she did of us girls. She tried hard to create a whole family

My Teens

again, even requesting we call Joe "Dad," but he would never be my father to me. However, all of us got along well. Joe was good to my mother and us. And for the 45 years she was married to him she had a companion for which I was grateful.

Joe, a widower, 41 years old, born in Russia, was the oldest of 6 children. He was an excellent nurse, having received his medical training when he served in the Army Corps in charge of a Field Hospital during the Spanish Insurrection after the Spanish American War in 1912. He continued his medical work in World War I and later ran the Hartford Dispensary, a clinic where patients could receive ongoing medical assistance. If his father had had money instead of a fish market, if there had been scholarships as there are today, Joe would have made a fine doctor, probably a surgeon. As it was, he sold insurance.

That fall, 1927, I returned to Norwich and lived with Mrs. Dembo, a relative of Aunt Goldie's husband. I had to complete a third year of my secondary language required for college entrance and Weaver High School in Hartford did not offer Greek instruction.

The Norwich Free Academy was and is an interesting secondary private day school. When the Academy was incorporated in 1854 as a private school by philanthropist John Fox Slater, all deserving Norwich students, whether rich or poor, received free tuition. Today, the Academy retains its own Board of Trustees which decides the curriculum, hires the faculty, care for the premises, and oversees the school's growth. The city of Norwich pays the tuition for each of its young people who attend. Also some neighboring communities choose to do the same.

I Remember Chesterfield

The Academy remains an unusual secondary school, especially known for its Fine Arts department and its adjunct Slater Museum. This single turreted and very handsome, muted red brick, three story high building was designed in Romanesque style by the then outstanding architect Stephen Earle of Worcester, Massachusetts and built by Flynt Building and Construction Company of the same city. On November 4, 1886, his son William Slater dedicated the Museum as a Memorial to his father, John Fox Slater. Their ancestor, Samuel Slater, had come from England, having memorized the formula for manufacturing textiles – it was illegal to export any secrets – and established the textile industry in America.

Slater Museum has an extensive and unusual cast collection of Greek, Roman and Renaissance sculptures providing a fine learning tool for Norwich Free Academy students.

There are only three such museums on the campus of a secondary school in the country. The years I attended NFA offered the Classical Division for students preparing to go to college, the General Division for those not going for further scholastic education and the Commercial Division or Business School. Freshmen were called *Juniors*; Sophomores were *Lower Middlers* and Juniors *Upper Middlers*. Seniors were *Seniors*.

I loved my days at the Academy. Especially the Greek and Latin studies that revealed new languages, new exciting worlds I had never imagined. Even to this day in my heart I cherish all that I remember about the golden days of Attic culture. I even won the Ancient History prize my Freshman year.

For three years as one of eleven students in Dr. Bunnell's Greek class, translating portions of the Iliad and the Odyssey remains one of my happiest memories. I can visualize Dr. Bunnell. Tall, lean, gray-haired and sweet tempered, his legs tucked under his chair, patiently listening to us interpret Homer's iambic hexameter epic poetry. Young, romantic and naïve, I was smitten by the love story of the daring Prince Paris who kidnapped the Greek Queen Helen of unending beauty and the ensuing tragic ten year war. I remember when Dr. Bunnell skipped the erotic passages describing Paris returning from battle to embrace Helen on their couch. He thought the contents were not for our innocent minds. I translated them anyhow.

I was fascinated by the conflicting human emotions, the fickle, fallible Gods, their petty jealousies and manipulations as they influenced the respective actions of their favorite heroes. The myths, the panoply of lesser deities – it all fired my imagination. Yet, not once, growing up in the small town of Norwich, did I ever envision visiting Greece.

❦ ❦

May, 1963.

Isi would say to me, "Let's get away. You decide."

I was delighted to make the arrangements. After one trip to England, another to Italy, I chose Greece. We would spend eight enchanted days in a land thousands of years old. A Trinity College professor suggested I plan to be there when the moon is full.

After dinner on a magnificent moonlit night, Isi and I left the brand new stunning Hilton Hotel where we were staying and for the second time that day picked our way up the hill through the scattered debris of historic chunks of marble and ancient stones until we reached the crest of the Acropolis, once the glory of Greece. Here Socrates and Plato had strolled, remarkable and gifted sculptors, scientists, philosophers and authors had passed. And now I. I was ecstatic, rapt in the ethereal beauty, the mystical aura of long ago. Amidst the dust of centuries and the ruins at our feet Isi and I stood alone, just the two of us, in the breathtakingly beautiful flood of opaque white light. Behind us loomed the resplendent columns of the Parthenon. Below us the city of Athens clung to its ancient soil. A soft breeze blowing in baby gusts teased my hair, tugged at my dress, whispered in my ears. I smiled. Was some Olympic God conversing with me?

"Pinch me," I said to Isi as we descended. "Pinch me. I can't believe I'm here. I can't believe this is real."

Even though I studied Greek with Dr. Bunnell for three years, even though I won the Ancient History prize my Freshman year at the Academy studying in Rosa Wilcox's class, did I ever dream that one day I would actually visit Greece?

As we drove up to Delphi in the brilliant sunshine of early morning the mountainsides were a riot of color. Millions of red poppies, white, blue and yellow wild flowers everywhere. Outside, around occasional tavernas sat a small group of men, dressed in somber black suits watching a young lamb roasting on a spit. Shapeless women, swathed in black and wearing white head cloths, bounced through the fields astride little burrows. I thought of Chesterfield.

I remember saying to Isi. "When I see these rural folk, farmers, I think of my grandparents. I feel so sorry for them. How hard they worked. They never had any fun. Never had any opportunity to travel as we are or see the world. All these wonderful places they didn't know even existed. Their lives were so difficult. They just worked and then died."

Isi consoled me. "They knew no differently, Micki. They lived as they expected to. Sure they worked hard. So did everybody else. Me too. Fortunately you never had to. But they did what they had to, like all the farmers in Chesterfield. They knew what was important for them and they did it as well as they could."

Once again Memory sidetracked me.

All of us students became good friends. Saul Sussman and I paired off. We shared many of the same English, Math and Latin classes too. Together we attended parties, sorority and fraternity social events, school dances, Proms. I still am amused as I think back to when he and I won first prize at a card party. We played whist before Contract Bridge evolved. "It was easy," he said to me later. "There was a mirror behind you and I could see all your cards."

I remember the June night after our Senior Prom. Only 3 AM, we decided to drive to the top of a hill Saul knew to watch the dawn creep in the sky and the sun rise. I remember how we sat and conjectured about what our futures would bring. I wanted the WORLD! All of it! With open arms I remember thinking, "I embrace you. Come. Let me feel you to my very depths. My hopes, my struggles, my achievements."

I Remember Chesterfield

Saul matriculated at Brown University in Providence, Rhode Island and I was accepted at Connecticut College in New London. When Saul came home to Norwich on weekends he would phone me and we would go out to dinner, then to a movie or a walk on the boardwalk at Ocean Beach. I loved the wind in my face, the damp salt air, the roll of the waves. I'd be thrilled as we stood at the end of the pier jutting out over the water. On a winter's night the buffeting wind was wild, the sea rough, the spray high. The spell of the calm silvery waters on a clear moonlit night was magic – awe-inspiring.

Saul and I, coming from a small school in an unsophisticated community, often discussed our similar reactions to the large institutions of learning where we met and lived with students from all over the States whose backgrounds were so diverse. I envied the students who had gone to resident private boarding prep schools. They knew the ropes that I had yet to learn.

I fondly remember my freshman year when I lived in Knowlton, an upper class dorm. Each evening we dressed for dinner, sang grace before we sat down to dine and were served our food. I was exposed to more formal table etiquette. Bread and butter plates. Seated at Dean Nye's table, I watched how daintily she quartered her dessert, a pear, then peeled each section and diced it into small pieces to be eaten with her fork. At the formal dances we wore long dresses and elbow length white gloves. My mother bought me beautiful outfits, a wine-colored velvet dress with a knockout rhinestone buckle to wear to the tea dances. Uncle Louis fashioned a gorgeous black lace gown for me and I bought a stunning floor length black skirt, white wrap-around blouse at Russek's Department Store in New York. If one of the C.C. girls did not have an escort to take to a dance, she could go and choose the most handsome man, tap his partner on the shoulder and claim him. I remember one heavyset girl who always did this, but not me.

In 1928 when I entered Connecticut College the school maintained an unusual restriction. The number of nights a student could spend off campus depended on her grades. Fortunately, my marks were high and each semester I had unlimited nights. Otherwise we had to be back at the dorm and sign in by 11 o'clock. When President Blunt assumed her office in 1929 smoking was allowed and the curfew was raised on Saturday nights to 1:00 A.M., much to Dean Burdick's puzzlement.

"What do you girls do?" she asked. "The movies are over by eleven." No one answered her.

When Saul and I had a date and I could stay off campus, he would drive me to Chesterfield. To be away from the grind was a delight. And I always enjoyed being with my grandparents. Grandma would wait up for us, even if it were midnight. We sat in the big cozy kitchen at the square table in the muted yellow glow of the kerosene lamps, the shiny aluminum kettle gently bubbling on the rear of the stove. Grandma served us tea in glasses, Russian style, and a tray of her pastries. We chatted for an hour or so. She liked Saul very much. He was kind, very smart in an understated manner, soft spoken, nice looking and courteous. He liked her too and looked forward to these midnight trysts.

When he left she would bring me one of her voluminous flannel nightgowns and I went to sleep in the miniature bedroom off the downstairs hall. As I snuggled down between the cold sheets, my head resting on a huge square pillow of the softest down, a

I Remember Chesterfield

lightweight *perineh* (down quilt) over me, I could have been any little Russian Jewish child tucked into bed by a doting grandmother in any small Russian village. For that was just what Chesterfield had been for the past 40 years, ever since the first Jewish settlers, aided by the Baron de Hirsch, bought farms there. They prepared and ate the same kinds of food they were accustomed to; they wallowed through comparable snowdrifts and plied their ways over frozen roads. They experienced a similar routine of daily physical effort and they prayed in the familiar religious cycles they knew so well. With one exception. No longer did they dread murderous pogroms. No longer did they suffer cruel man-made laws. Chesterfield was the promise they had hoped for, strove after.

The Summer That Changed My Life
Chapter XII

Little did I anticipate that I would spend the summer of 1931 in Chesterfield and meet the man I was to marry.

Early in June I returned to Hartford and again was experiencing the sharp transitional adjustment from school to home, not easy for me. My junior year at Connecticut College was complete. Only one more year to go and then I'd be up and out on my own! "Watch my dust," I would think. I knew I didn't want to teach and I was sure I didn't want to be a counselor at camp again. But decisions could wait. Now the summer loomed ahead to rest and read.

However, my mother was annoyed with me. "Why don't you get a job?" she challenged me one afternoon.

A job, I thought. The last thing on my mind! The country's in the throes of a severe depression. Even men can't find work. I had heard that at Macy's Department Store in New York college graduates were working as sales personnel. And who would hire me just for the summer? A Liberal Arts major, my brain crammed with literature centuries old ... I had no training for any clerical position, although I had signed up for typing and accounting next semester.

"So what'll I do?" I answered her, "wrap packages in some dinky store like Joe's niece for $2 a day?"

"But what will you do," she demanded, "all summer? Just loaf?"

I couldn't see myself at home! "I'll go to Chesterfield," I said. "I'd like to do nothing for a while. I'm tired. I studied hard last year."

"And what will you do on the farm?"

I Remember Chesterfield

"The usual. Don't worry, I've got gobs of reading to do for a course in Continental Lit and I told you, Jeanette's invited me to go upstate New York with her parents for two weeks in July. When I come back I'll go to Grandma's for the rest of the summer. Maybe she'd like company. Aunt Rose isn't going to be there."

My mother had no reply. She knew I had decided. I would not work in any hot crowded department store and I really didn't want to stay in Hartford.

Living on the farm was lovely. I settled in the little bedroom at the top of the stairs. Aunt Helen had married and was ensconced in the apartment over the store. Uncle Jake and Aunt Doris occupied a house in the village. I still enjoyed swimming in Kosofski's brook and berrying. Saul had promised to come down and I had a few dates lined up with people who lived in New London. At night I usually joined the crowd at the store. I was not unhappy because I knew I was marking time until I graduated and would be free.

One morning near the end of July when I came down to breakfast, I found Tillie sitting at Grandma's table with a deck of cards in her hand. Tillie came from New York with her two young sons for the summer and was Grandpa's only paying roomer. Her sharp face, the shape of her body, her drab clothes reminded me of a perky little brown hen.

"What are you doing with cards so early in the morning?" I asked her. She looked so forlorn.

"I've nothing else to do. The boys are somewhere with your grandfather. Want me to tell your fortune?"

I poured my coffee and sat down. "I don't believe such nonsense." I laughed. "But go ahead if you want to."

The Summer That Changed My Life

She spread the cards. "There's a dark man in your life who loves you."

I laughed again. "There's no such man, no man I know is dark and no man's in love with me."

But she insisted. "Look here. The Jack of Spades facing you, the Queen of Spades, and the hearts, the love cards, all around."

"So what?" I was amused.

"The cards don't lie, Micki."

"You're just romantic, Tillie."

By the time I had finished breakfast I had agreed to walk down to the store with her after supper.

I remember the pretty pongee yellow dress with black braid around the neckline I wore that night. While I was in college my mother bought me beautiful, expensive clothes. Maybe because she didn't consider I was attractive I needed them. Often when I'd be trying clothes on she'd say to me, "From the back, Mildred, you look beautiful." Or, perhaps, she enjoyed seeing me well dressed. But I liked the way my clothes looked from the front. Now as I study my college picture I wasn't homely at all, 5'5", thin, nice features, clear skin and an easy smile. I didn't resemble her family, all of whom were comely. Nor was I the dimply, darling cutesy that Libby was. I was more reserved. I looked like my father's family whom my mother disdained.

The store had a good crowd the night I meandered down with Tillie. All the regulars were there including the wives of three New York families, the Anapolskys, Greenbergs and Grodinskys, who had built summer homes on the road beyond my grandparents' farm. As we milled around, the conversation was light. I didn't have much in

I Remember Chesterfield

common with these people; my background was too different, but I liked them and the evening promised to be pleasant.

About 9 o'clock Isi drove up. He slammed the brakes so hard, so quickly, the car rocked on its wheels. I watched him as he strolled into the store. I hadn't seen him for a couple of years. He had grown taller, his shoulders had broadened. Black hair, straight as an Indian's, brushed back off his forehead. Black eyes, deep set. He smiled quietly as he greeted several people who approached him. Not I. I stood where I was. I noticed his face was tanned and healthy looking. Under his blue shirt and khaki trousers his body appeared well muscled. I was surprised to see how he had changed.

It took him 10 minutes to make his way to me. I remember this clearly.

"Hello, Micki. How are your?"

"Okay. And how are you?"

"Good, thanks. I heard you were in Chesterfield this summer."

"That's right." I was nonchalant.

"I've been down to the store a few times looking for you."

That surprised me. "Well, I was away for a bit, but I'm here now until I go back to school in September. But what are you doing in Chesterfield? Someone told me you were working for you brother Butch."

"I am. Butch's got a job at Spruce Lodge building a dam, so I'm living at home until it's finished."

"Where's Spruce Lodge?"

"It's a small hotel in Yantic. The owners are damming a brook to make a swimming pool."

I knew Yantic was on the outskirts of Norwich.

The Summer That Changed My Life

Isi, Bulkeley High School, 1927

I Remember Chesterfield

"That's nice," I said.

"What to go for a ride?" He sounded casual, but I sensed he wasn't. There was this tension about him. Later I was to recognize this same controlled tightness whenever he was anxious.

"Sure." I was glad to go. "Just let me tell Aunt Helen where I'm going so she won't worry."

The top of Isi's green Ford roadster with a rumble seat was down. He held the door for me and we were off. He drove fast over roads that were strange to me but obviously he knew well. The mild summer night tore at me. I took the pins out of my long hair and let the rushing breeze buffet my face, my body. Heady scents of new mown hay and honeysuckle. We sped through darkness.

We were silver bullets streaking through the sky.

We were shooting stars skimming the heavens.

We were blazing comets bursting through silent space.

I don't know how long Isi drove. Finally he slowed down, turned onto a bumpy country lane and stopped.

I sat up, pushed the hair off my face and asked, "Where are we? I hear water."

"We're near Bond's brook. Do you want to see it?"

Bond's brook meant nothing to me but I said "Sure."

Hand in hand, we walked over the uneven ground. I saw the miniature waterfall froth with foam, tumble over the big scattered rocks in its path, surge and swirl as it rushed on under a makeshift bridge of wooden planks and disappear into the darkness. Two tall trees, straight as sentinels, stood side by side at the edge of the clearing. I questioned Isi about the noise I was hearing.

"They're katydids," he answered. "Listen. Katydid, katydid, katydid. They sing all night."

"Funny. We just called them tree frogs."

Back in the car Isi said, "Come closer," and I slid into the circle of his arm. I noticed the pleased smile creep into his eyes. We talked. He, about how difficult it had been at Buckley Academy in New London, he was the only one left on the farm with his mother and there were endless chores. "I wanted to play football, but if I missed the bus it's a 10 mile walk home." He wanted to go to college, but it meant his mother would have to continue taking boarders and so he went to work for Butch who had recently established a business constructing roads and bridges. Education was not high on the Savin list of success. Earning money was. This they did well.

The small glade where Isi had parked the car soon became our very own favorite place. I smile as I remember how ethereal and elegant the little clearing shone on brilliant moonlit nights, the naked trees like knights sheathed in silver. Twinkling stars strung out like tiaras of diamonds among the branches. How snug and secluded we felt in the warm car on frigid winter nights.

Then there was the night Isi had to drive to the Bronx in New York to pick up a part for a piece of equipment that had unexpectedly broken down and needed to be repaired immediately. Would I go with him? We left after supper and reached our destination about midnight. There were no super highways then, just good-old twisting U.S. 1. Dawn was breaking when we arrived back in Chesterfield. Pretty tired, we sat in the car and watched the miracle of the sky lightening. Darkness began to fade, the trees slowly took shape, the buildings gradually emerged. The haunting plaint of a single whip-

I Remember Chesterfield

poor-will pierced the quiet. I can still recall the fatigue I felt, sense the serenity of the early sweet summer morning, hear once again the mournful whip-poor-will, whip-poor-will.

Isi and I dated frequently the rest of the summer. Along the seashore, an easy drive from Chesterfield, there were several popular restaurants, good movies and the theater at Ivoryton, so named because ivory keys for pianos were manufactured there. Chairs were setup in the Ivoryton Town Hall and each week, under the sponsorship of Milton Steifel, a different drama was presented by touring stock companies. I remember we saw Katherine Hepburn at the onset of her career.

The first time Isi invited me to come home with him fell on *Rosh Hashonah*, the Jewish New Year, in September. We walked the long mile from the little synagogue slowly, then up the wide stone steps into the house. A loud chorus greeted us.

"Where have you been? What took you so long? We waited for you. Hurry Up. We're starved."

Quickly we took our places at the table. Isi introduced me to his mother whom I recognized, his sister Bess and her husband Abe, Isi's brother Moe and his wife Edith, his brother Butch and his wife Anne and four grandchildren. I didn't realize I was the first girl Isi had brought home. Nor did I understand that their jocularity and teasing expressions masked their fondness for him, their baby brother.

I remember how impressed, even surprised, I was as I glanced around the huge dining room, maybe 20 feet across. My mother-in-law to be always considered the dining room the most important in a house. Wallpaper with large colorful blossoms, a massive single hearthstone slab under a brown upright stove for

The Summer That Changed My Life

heating, starched white curtains crisscrossed on four large windows, begonias bloomed in coffee cans. Most significant was the extended table holding the twelve of us. A spotless white linen cloth, polished silverware, matched plates and shining silver-stemmed wine goblets. In Chesterfield I had not seen this formality, this space. Abe chanted the blessing over bread, the *kiddush* over wine and the prayer to God, of thankfulness for having brought us to this happy day. A restless child spilled his wine. Everyone laughed and the party began. Mrs. Savin, whom I shall hereafter call Mama, served a gargantuan dinner.

The animated conversation around the table fascinated me. The men discussed current politics, the coming election, their business problems, what went on at the synagogue service that morning, which congregant bought which honor, even how Mrs. Wickson's cow got lost in the woods last week and the trouble they had finding her. Beyond my college walls and except for my Dartmouth friends, I had not heard such knowledgeable and interesting conversation before, especially in Chesterfield.

Back at school Isi and I continued to date two and three times a week. My requirements were low. I had unlimited nights. The weeks flew.

Isi loved to drive. We took our first foliage trip over the Mohawk Trail and into Vermont to view the glorious colors, the stunning vistas. I also remember how dismayed I felt in Vermont noticing the obvious effects of the Depression, shabby, run down, neglected properties. On porches wood stacked high against the coming winter, worn clothing strung out to dry, rubbish filled yards.

I Remember Chesterfield

I soon realized how deeply Isi loved me. I could tell by the light in his eyes, his tender gestures, his many considerations and how hard he endeavored to please me. But the only man I would marry, I told him one night as we sat in the car near our little brook, would be the one I loved. I didn't love him then.

"Things are changing for women," I remember saying to him. "You don't have to be only a nurse or a secretary or a teacher any more. There are other opportunities. When I finish school the first thing I want to do is to travel." I would be receiving my inheritance in February and a trip to Europe beckoned me. "I want to see what I can do." I didn't tell him that in my Composition class recently the Professor had read one of my stories and then said, "This girl can write." But being an author never crossed my mind. Writing was no career.

However, I couldn't fail to appreciate what an unusual person Isi was and how all encompassing and profound was his love for me. I needed to be loved like that, completely, and to love someone with all my heart. The silent ache of the loss of my father lay deep within me.

When I was home in Hartford during the Christmas – New Year's break from school Isi had phoned to ask me to accompany him on a trip upstate to deliver some Christmas gifts for Butch. I remember that afternoon. No sun, sullen gray clouds threatened. Patches of snow lay in crevices along the highway. But in the little Ford roadster it was cozy as we drove, Isi's right arm held me close to him. At one of the last stops he left the motor running for heat, tucked the robe across my lap and under my knees and said, "I won't be long." When he had gone I sat there and realized I loved him too, how cherished I was, how protected I felt with him, how much I needed his strength and love. When Isi returned to the car I told him I loved him. I would spend the rest of my life with him. It was a decision I never regretted, although I have to admit there were to be trying times ahead. He was thrilled, of course. We celebrated with dinner by candlelight at an Inn somewhere in Massachusetts.

The following week we went to New York to select my diamond solitaire which I designed. It probably took his last dollar. We saw *Mourning Becomes Electra* and Isi said everyone in New London knew Eugene O'Neill was an old drunk (He is also one of America's greatest playwrights.) On New Year's Eve we attended the newly opened Bushnell Memorial in Hartford to watch Ted Shawn and Ruth St. Dennis dance. During exams in January Isi drove from Hope, Rhode Island, where he was working to take me from college to Hartford, a 100-mile trip, to hear Paderewski on his final American concert tour.

On January 10, 1932 my mother and Joe held an engagement party for us. I knew only a few of their friends and remember little of the affair. But the dress I wore was my favorite, a simple unadorned magenta silk crepe that fell softly midcalf. It had a bateau neckline and a chartreuse sash, which I draped around my waist. Isi sent me a white orchid.

For my birthday, February 24, – I was 21 and could vote! – Isi sent me the most magnificent American Beauty red roses, which he continued to do on my every birthday and holiday with little notes "to my sweetheart." Those roses arrived in a box nearly as tall as myself. "You've got some boyfriend," the florist, whom I knew, said to me later. "We had to send to New York for those flowers." When they

I Remember Chesterfield

faded, I snipped the buds, put them in the empty Valentine box of candy Isi had given me and saved them for years.

As I am writing these memories, it is spring and my handsome lilac bushes are in enchanting bloom. It is raining quietly, a misty cool morning the Irish call a soft morning, dull gray skies overcast with cheerless dense clouds. The same kind of morning as on the Sunday in mid-May, 1932, when Isi came to take me to Devil's Hopyard in Salem which I had wanted to see. This natural wonder, only four miles from Chesterfield, turned out to be a decent sized waterfall that cascaded and swirled over the hollowed tops of huge boulders strewn about. Legend claims the Devil was so mad that day when he hopped on them his fire gouged impressive holes in the surfaces of the rocks.

When we left we drove over a narrow, rain-drenched road through a forest. As we came up a long grade and just reached the crest the sun peeked out. Instantly the entire woods changed. The world became chartreuse! Black were the wet trunks of the trees. Black were the branches. Black were the tiny twigs. And every young, glistening, rain-splattered green leaf turned to gold. A strange sight. A strange color. Awed, Isi stopped the car. We sat silent, unbelieving the rare phenomenon we were witnessing. It lasted but a short while. The sun slid away, disappeared. Thick clouds closed and our enchanted world was no more. Slowly Isi drove down the other side of the hill. At its bottom I spied a stand of lilac trees in full array, bending over a gaping cellar hole where once a dwelling had stood, and some nostalgic wife had planted her favorite shrubs.

"Look at those lilacs," I gasped.

"Want some?"

The Summer That Changed My Life

Knee deep through the sodden grasses Isi waded and brought me an enormous bunch of lilacs. I buried my face in their heavy, exotic scent and never forgot the thrill. Since that day in May I always tried to recapture that memorable moment, to once again glimpse a green-golden wet woods. Only one time, in all my years, after Isi died, did I experience another. On that June morning, just after dawn, I stood barefoot in my nightgown on the wet deck of our new home, breathing deep of the fragrant damp air. It had rained through the night. The treetops at my eye level sagged with moisture. A mass of leaden clouds hugged the horizon and covered the eastern sky. Suddenly, a cloud shifted. The sky opened and the rising sun flung its golden rays into the woods below me. The trees turned chartreuse! Black were the tree trunks. Gleaming black were the branches, black the wee twigs. And every little, dripping, twittering leaf glistened with gold. I held my breath in disbelief, elated. The phenomenon for which I had long sought actually re-occurred. I couldn't believe it, the miracle I had waited years to once again behold. The scene lingered but a moment and was gone. Dark clouds merged and covered the sky. But the memory of that thrilling glimpse of a chartreuse forest on that singular day in May when Isi and I drove back from Devil's Hopyard to Chesterfield, the glorious perfume of water laden, lush lilacs, has never left me.

I Remember Chesterfield

Grandmother Sarah Kaplan

My Grandmother
Chapter XIII

If I were to choose one word to characterize my maternal grandmother Sarah Kaplan it would be patience, infinite, unquestioning patience. When I consider what her years in Chesterfield on the farm must have been, her demanding life, her silent suffering and physical endurance, I am filled with awe and admiration.

Nothing was easy. Buckets overflowing with water hauled in from an outside well, hot water in a tank on the side of a wood burning stove requiring frequent stoking. Freezing bedrooms in winter. Suffocating heat in summer. Yet I never heard her raise her voice in anger or frustration, never argue with anyone or utter a complaint. I never saw her weep and if she were bitter at any time, there was no manifestation. But then I never saw her smile either – or heard her laugh. Meek she wasn't. She had to possess plenty of spunk and fortitude to have survived her ordeals. Quietly, patiently she bore her burdens with stoicism and each night massaged her aching limbs with Dickinson's Witch Hazel.

Born in 1869, she was 18 years old when she married my grandfather John Kaplan and came to America. In the first 10 years of marriage she gave birth to seven children, five girls, two boys. What was it like for her I ask myself? How did she bathe them with no plumbing? Wash their heavy winter clothes indoors? She had no help. They were too poor to afford any. How did she feed them all? I can hear my mother speak when my sister Libby refused to eat

I Remember Chesterfield

something, "You don't know what it is to be hungry. Growing up, we were so hungry all of us kids would cling to Grandma's skirts and watch her as she dropped the egg and flour mixture into the boiling milk that was to be our supper." My mother always set great store by food.

Grandma was a pretty woman, despite endless tasks, crushing tasks. She maintained a strong personal pride. With the years her body thickened and grew shorter. I remember how I measured myself against her, first up to her shoulders, then as tall as she was, and then – voila!, taller than her 5'5" height. Her long dark hair – I never saw it uncombed – held its lustrous quality and color to the end when it just began to turn gray at the temples. Soft and unwrinkled was her fair skin, faintly tinged with rose and unblemished. I'm sure the warm moisture emanating from the big aluminum kettle simmering at the rear of the stove must have been a benefit as well as the Pond's cold cream she used, her only cosmetic. Often she warned me, "Never put hot water on your face," and I don't. Unlike some of the farmers' wives, she didn't garden or enter the barn to milk or gather eggs in the hen house. Grandma was an immaculate person and concerned about her appearance. Her light colored housedresses and aprons were starched and unspotted. Much to her credit she enjoyed the first full indoor bathroom in Chesterfield, tub and all.

Grandma's one great sadness happened when I was in the fifth grade, about 1920. My darling Uncle Ben, whom I liked so much, left Chesterfield. I can remember the anguish we all felt. After the war he had studied at the University of Connecticut Agricultural College. Coming back to the farm, he tried to convince my Grandfather to

My Grandmother

improve his farming techniques. My hotheaded Grandfather became infuriated. There must have been a big row. Ben picked up and moved to California, never to return. For a short time the family knew where he was. At my mother's request I wrote him childish letters which he never answered. Soon he severed all family contacts, changed his name, married and moved to a new address. My Grandmother must have been devastated. Something in her must have died and I'm sure she mourned him all her life. But I never heard her speak of him. There was no use. She buried her loss in the privacy of her heartache. Aunt Rose, when she moved to California, did track him down. Ben met her secretly once but he had no wish to resume any relationships. I never saw him again.

After I was married and learning to cook, how often I would think about the meals we were served at school. All of us girls griped about creamed celery, repetitive menus and stayed away whenever we could on Friday nights when fish and pie were served. But, in retrospect, I decided the food wasn't so bad. And I would remember Grandma when I was in my teens. She was a fabulous cook. Her rosy-cream borscht was lovely to behold and nectar-like to consume. Now, I rationalize. The beets were organically grown, the beaten eggs, added to the hot soup so carefully as not to curdle, were laid that morning, the sweet cream was unadulterated and unpasteurized. She used a bit of sour salt. Served on a hot summer day, sometimes with a boiled potato, nothing was more delicious than her cold borscht.

I Remember Chesterfield

Her *gefilte* fish was the best I ever tasted, even though she purchased the less expensive fish. She'd sit on a Friday morning in her kitchen near the window and with her small, wooden handled iron tool, chop the fish in her little wooden bowl for two hours, adding cold water bit by bit, never a filler, until the fine consistency pleased her. Placing carrots, onions and fish bones in an enamel pan, she laid the fish balls over them, added water and simmered them until done. When they came to the table, each serving of fish, decorated with a carrot circle on top, could have been a picture in a magazine.

The *matzoh brei* she made every Passover I try to emulate but it never tastes the same as hers. Pouring boiling water from the big aluminum kettle onto the *matzoh* crumpled in a bowl to soften them, she drained the water, added beaten eggs, perhaps a little sugar, then sautéed the mixture in her sweet butter as a large pancake. Somehow she saved cranberries from the fall and served the *matzoh brei* with cranberry preserves. She also made a marvelous chunky quince preserve! I always search for it in specialty stores and never have found its equal.

Grandma concocted a superb noodle pudding, commonly called *kugel*. To the cooked noodles she had prepared herself, she added clotted cream, sugar, eggs, her own farmer cheese, butter, raisins or apples and cinnamon, mixed them and baked it all in a casserole until the pudding was firm enough to cut and a bit brown and crispy on top.

When the fish peddler would drive up on the yard once or twice a week she would choose flounder, only a nickel a pound, which probably had been swimming in New London Bay that morning. The peddler would scale, gut and slice the fish. For supper that night she would dip the fish in flour and egg and fry it slowly in the sweet butter she had churned. Even the flesh clinging to the bones was toothsome. The lingering memory of Grandma's fish prevents me from buying the soulless flounder fillets I see in the market today.

Did everything taste so good because it was so slowly cooked and the flavors had time to develop? Unfortunately, I have no recipes of hers. I wasn't interested in cooking when I visited the farm and she may not have been able to give me any. She didn't use measurements the way we do today. I remember how she peeled cored and quartered apples in the fall and dried them in a net hung above the stove. The homemade farmer cheese that dripped overnight through a cloth bag. How she wrapped a herring in a newspaper and inserted it near the flue of the stove, just beyond the flames of the fire. When the paper charred, she removed the fish which was similar to having been broiled. I didn't like herring, but other people savored it. When we lived in Greeneville, I remember how we looked forward to Friday mornings in the winter when the mailman would deliver a package from Grandma. In it were my favorite flavorsome small twisted rolls we called *fagalach*, "little birds."

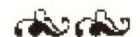

Grandma was a woman of few words. To me she spoke a well-pronounced English. I wouldn't have understood anything else. We didn't have long discussions or heart-to-heart talks. Our affection

I Remember Chesterfield

and understanding were tacit. Yet one very significant conversation I can never forget.

On a lovely Saturday morning in April 1932, when I was spending the weekend in Chesterfield, we sat by ourselves in her bright kitchen. Through the big windows sunlight streamed on either side of the square table draped with its Sabbath cloth. On it stood her ornate, five candle silver candelabra over which she had recited the Sabbath blessing the night before. We had just finished playing Duroc, a game of cards I think must have been a version of Old Maid because we sent cards back and forth.

I was happy that morning, very much in love, engaged to be married in June after college graduation. So I was surprised when, for the first time, she mentioned misgivings about my coming marriage to Isi. She must have pondered over them for a long time before she spoke.

I knew what she meant. Nobody except my mother sanctioned my future husband, a poor farm boy. In both my mother and father's families I was the first grandchild who would attain a college degree. They all desired me to choose a man of comparable prestige, education and financial security. Aunt Dora, my Dad's sister, who lived in Norwich and whom I would visit, suggested that I, with my inheritance and background, could do better. "A doctor maybe." "I should wait a little." My future mother-in-law was greatly disturbed. Years later she confessed to me that she, who put great validity in dreams, had dreamed she should stop this marriage. She felt Isi, her youngest, last unmarried child, was marrying out of his league and she feared that I could not, would not, adapt to the simple kind of life he offered me.

And my Grandmother. I understood her too. There was no great friendship or relationship between her and Mrs. Savin. They seldom saw each other. She wasn't like Mrs. Miller and Mrs. Leviloff who walked from the village on a Saturday afternoon to visit my Grandmother for a glass of tea and some gossip. I used to chuckle as I overheard their conversations comparing and bragging about the various achievements of their respective children and grandchildren.

Nor did Grandma approve of the way Isi drove. Whenever he came to call for me he drove up on the yard fast, then slammed on the brakes so hard the car literally shuddered in its tracks. "Does he always drive like that?" she asked me one day, "or does he have a car specially built?"

"He drives like that," I answered her. She must have been displeased, but said nothing.

Isi did not come into the house to woo her. He was always in a rush to go. She did not know him as well as she did Saul, whom she liked so much.

"Well," I answered my Grandmother's misgiving flippantly, "I can always get a divorce."

She stood up, gazed out the window and finally spoke.

"Divorce isn't so easy."

I was startled. What did she know about divorce? It wasn't so prevalent in 1932, although the new idea, Companionate Marriage, had created an impression and created contention. And, being on a farm with scant exposure to the outside world? Would she have preferred divorce, I wondered, to the hardships she had undergone? Under traditional Jewish law only a husband can initiate divorce. A wife has few rights. Furthermore, a divorced woman was a great disgrace, a discard, unworthy, frowned upon, disrespected, with no place in society. I remember how derisively Mrs. Savin spoke when one of her friend's sons married a divorced woman. No dishonor could be worse. So Grandma could never get a divorce. She had no options. But she wanted more for me than she had.

But I knew the person I was marrying and I loved him. For the first time since my father died I felt safe in Isi's embrace, secure, truly loved. He is the only person in the world, I thought, who loves me unequivocally and I hungered for that kind of love. I realized I needed his strength, moral and physical — he could break an apple in half with his bare hands — his street smarts — I had only book knowledge — his wisdom, his tenderness. I discerned the goodness in his heart, the depth of his emotion he could never articulate, his generosity, his loyalty, I was not afraid to face my future with him. And I knew he would not be poor all his life.

Except for a miniature picture of her, the only memento I have of Grandma is a round Majolica salad plate which she kept on a shelf in the kitchen's small dish closet where she hid her *knippel*. I love that word *knippel*, even its sound. Actually, it means a knot. Women kept their pin money in the knot of a handkerchief. I like to think of a *knippel* as a woman's private financial resource. I believe every woman should have her own *knippel*, a kind of independence. I don't know how much Grandma had or how she acquired it, but she always gave us gifts of five to ten dollar gold pieces. They were legal then.

My Grandmother

My beautiful, loving grandmother sat up in bed one November day in 1932, five months after I was married, and fell back, never to rise again. She was only 63 years old. I regret I didn't know her long enough.

I don't remember going to her funeral. I probably didn't go. Isi and I were living in Catskill, New York at the time and when Isi informed me of her death it was too late. Even if he had driven me to Chesterfield, she would have been buried. Orthodox Jewish people believe in quick burials.

I don't know what happened to Grandma's possessions. She had some lovely things. Aunt Rose took most of her jewelry to New York and it was stolen later. I wanted Grandma's heavy gold wedding ring, but I realized it really belonged to Aunt Helen whose daughter Barbara now possesses it.

However, I hold dear a wealth of memories. I easily conjure vivid pictures of Grandma, sitting in the chair by the sunny kitchen window, lifting the heavy aluminum kettle as she prepared something, quietly resting in the late afternoon before beginning chores for supper, bathing in the small brook flowing through the meadow across the narrow lane from the farm. Memories of her remarkable culinary skill. Memories of her patient, silent devotion. Memories of her love.

I Remember Chesterfield

Micki, Connecticut College, 1932

The Transition
Chapter XIV

Graduation Day, June 13, 1932. A very memorable day.

In the morning, clear and sunny, happy girls of the Junior class, dressed in white, like Vestal virgins I thought, carried a long chain woven of white daisies down the aisle. We, about to graduate, in caps and gowns, followed them and took our places on the platform. Was I excited? Exhilarated? At last I had completed 17 years of Academia! When I transferred the tassel on my cap to the other side, when I took my diploma in hand, I had achieved one of my childhood goals. My father would have been pleased. Now I was independent, educated, free and eager to enter a new phase of my life.

In the afternoon Isi and I drove into Hartford to obtain our marriage license. Then I met my mother and we found a lovely, plain, white lace silk dress that clung to my body and gracefully fell full length. An unusually deep, detachable Bertha collar draped from my shoulders. I was ready.

Before our wedding I had a little fuss with Isi when I told him I did not want to take the vow – I was serious about this – to love, honor and obey. He was upset at changing the traditional, proscribed oath, but he did not protest. How pleased I was when Rabbi Silverman, to whom I had not spoken about this, asked me if I would love, honor and cherish Isi, I smiled to myself and answered "Yes." Things had changed.

I Remember Chesterfield

We held the small wedding at home, midafternoon, on Tuesday, June 21, 1932. I wore Aunt Doris's white veil and carried a spray of white roses. My stepfather Joe, who prided himself on his culinary skills, offered to prepare the dinner and that was fine with me.

I knew my mother-in-law was upset. She said so. She wanted a big, gala affair where people would dance around her as she, *jeddis baba*, celebrated the marriage of her last child. More importantly, she firmly believed that a splendid wedding boded well for the couple. It set the tone for their marriage.

But how could I plan a large wedding? I was away at school. I had no car. No license, although Isi had taught me to drive. My mother backed off from becoming involved, as she was wont to do. She didn't like to assume this kind of responsibility. Furthermore, she informed me, I would have to pay for everything out of my inheritance. I was loath to squander a large sum of money on a party, particularly in the Depression when finances were so precarious. And, Aunt Molly, my mother's next younger sister, pretty with dark hair and eyes, the most intelligent of the five sisters I thought, had died six weeks previously after a long bout with breast cancer. Only 40 years old, she was the first of the siblings to go. She left two small children.

I insisted my mother invite my father's family from Norwich. She didn't object. Some of them came. If they were uncomfortable they didn't say. However, my mother asked me when I released the publicity to the newspapers to state that I was the daughter of Mr. and Mrs. Joseph Rudy. I did, because I realized how much she wanted us to be known in the community as a complete family.

The Transition

For our honeymoon of five days we motored to Lake George, the Thousand Islands in Canada, where it was freezing cold, and back to Catskill, New York where, on Monday morning, Isi would be working on Butch's new project. Building a dam.

I was relieved not to be establishing a home right away, with furniture and all. We would be living in furnished apartments for a while and I liked the idea of getting to know other places beside Chesterfield, Norwich, New London and Hartford.

But I was lost in Catskill, a small town of 5,000 inhabitants, culturally stagnant in the Depression. Except for the movie house, Catskill was ARTS devoid! There was nothing for me to do. Gone now were the academia I loved, the stimulation of being with my peers at school, the horseback riding I enjoyed. I kept my boots and jodhpurs for the longest time, but never wore them again. Gone were the fun dates, the dinners and dancing, the cultural events Isi and I had attended, the short trips to interesting places.

And Isi worked. Heart and soul. President Roosevelt had inaugurated the WPA. One shift of men worked 10 hours a day, 50 cents an hour, for three days. Another shift the next three days. My husband covered both shifts. He was out of the house, often 14 hours a day, six days a week. During the two summers we stayed in Catskill, we drove only once to the State Capitol in Albany, 40 miles north, just to see it, although people frequently went there for anything they really wanted.

The first furnished house we rented, sight unseen, was out of town, isolated, high on a hill, elegant. When I walked out the French doors on either side of the long, lovely living room I beheld a sweeping panorama of countryside. The open sky, clean fresh air and greenery reminded me of Chesterfield. There wasn't much for me to do except to wait for Isi to come home. So I read a lot. The excellent library in the house had a good selection of books. I remember my pleasure when I, romantic me, discovered *The Sheik* and devoured it. I was too young to have seen Valentino in the movie.

I am still amused as I remember how I baked my first pie. Isi possessed a very sweet tooth. A week after we were living in Catskill Isi brought home a handbasket full of New York's famous, delicious, plump red cherries.

"Can you bake a pie?" he asked.

Not daunted, the next day I opened my Fanny Farmer cookbook, a gift from two of my classmates, and found the recipe for cherry pie. The crust rolled out with no problem. I pitted the cherries and then I read "dredge the cherries with flour." The only dredge I knew of was something used to dredge a river! I skipped that part. The stove in the kitchen was a relic, an ancient wood burning thing. Well, I thought, if Grandma could do so well with hers, I ought to be able to do the same. The recipe called for a 450-degree oven. On a perfectly beautiful July summer day I stood in the kitchen and shoved wood after wood into the stove. But the gauge never moved beyond 200 degrees. Disgusted and impatient, I put the pie in the oven anyhow. Soon after, the top crust turned a lovely brown ... the pie had to be done.

That night I served the pie. With a great anticipation and a big smile Isi cut into the crust. Cherry juice ran everywhere. The bottom crust was raw. It had never baked. He was so disappointed he just said nothing but took the pie, serving plate and all, walked out onto

The Transition

the porch and flung it as far as he could into the distance where it must have landed in the valley.

I was merely amused at his reaction.

We lived in that luxurious home for only a month. There was a $100 discrepancy between what the real estate agent told us and the rental money the owners expected. I found another small, furnished apartment off Main Street in Catskill and we moved.

Now I tried to fill my time while Isi worked and worked. I played bridge with the wives of the engineers who were in charge of the dam, but the women were older and settled. The Jewish matrons whom I met were kind, but we had little in common. What could we talk about? I had no children, no maid problems and I knew no recipes.

Every Sunday, come Hell or high water, wherever we were living, every holiday, American or Jewish, we drove to Chesterfield to Isi's mother for dinner.

From Catskill we crossed the Hudson River by ferry – the Rip Van Winkle Bridge had not yet been built – to Troy, New York. The road ran sharply uphill through the Red Light district. We could see the prostitutes lounging in the doorways or through their windows. Then on to Great Barrington, Massachusetts and all across the State of Connecticut to Chesterfield, a good two-hour trek, to spend the afternoon eating an enormous meal and visiting.

Writing "high water" reminds me of the Sunday night in December when we were returning from Chesterfield and the ferry at Troy wasn't in operation. Too much ice running in the river. We sped to Coxacki, 12 miles north, hoping to catch the last ferry there. Fortunately it was still in service. I stood on the deck in the moonless, starless dark night, fascinated and fearful, watching the prow cut across the rapidly flowing, angry current of black water. Swirling good-sized chunks of thick ice constantly bumped, bumped, bumped against the wooden ferry. I thought of the slave Eliza in *Uncle Tom's Cabin* as she fled her captivity. I felt as frightened as she was. I was afraid we would capsize.

I can honestly say that once married, I never enjoyed Chesterfield in the same capacity as I had. My grandmother was an irreplaceable memory. After she died I never drove back to her house again. No longer did I go for a refreshing swim in Kosofski's delightful brook. I really couldn't leave the Savin family after Mama's enormous dinners. Never again did I drive down to Aunt Helen's store in the evening to dally away a few hours with the Chesterfield people I knew. I felt I had entered the Savin Compound, a family sufficient unto themselves, devoted to each other and happy to be together. And Mama engineered that often. I was to learn how invisible and indestructible were the bonds of sympathy, loyalty, love and duty she had woven in her offspring.

Some of the times in the early years of my marriage were difficult for me. The transition from being independent and the oldest in my family to being the young wife of the youngest son (who naturally didn't know anything), my naïveté and inexperience in the non academic world and having to adapt to a less affluent environment all tested my always too little patience, but I listened and learned. It was three years before I complained to Isi and asked if we could do something else, at least on one Sunday. We did. He always tried to please me.

I remember how distraught and upset I was the first winter we were married. The job in Catskill had shut down. We relinquished the apartment in January and came to stay at Mama's big house. I hated it. It was so cold in that house. I came into the kitchen one morning to find that a pail of standing water had frozen solid overnight. I was appalled. Isi was accustomed to this. He grew up, as did all the Chesterfield children, sleeping in icy bedrooms, dashing from warm beds into the kitchens, once the stoves had been lit. Mama wore felt boots and under her long wool skirt probably six petticoats. I, in my thin silk nightgowns, short skirts and leather shoes, shivered even though the portable kerosene heater, the kitchen and dining room stoves struggled valiantly against the frigid, paralyzing below zero temperature. Mama tried so hard to make me comfortable, but I was miserable.

In the late 1920's the utility company had electrified the rural area of Chesterfield. My grandparents had electric lights. Aunt Helen no longer polished sooty kerosene lamp chimneys. They even installed an oil burning, hot air furnace. But not my mother-in-law. Mama clung to her familiar ways. Years before, she was the only one I knew in Chesterfield who had installed a generator in her big house to provide power for electric illumination. The damn generator was always breaking down. Many a night before we were married I sat and waited in silence while Isi tinkered with it. Then, when it was running again, it was too late to go anywhere except to New London for an ice cream sundae.

In June 1933, after Mitchell was born, we returned to Catskill where Isi was already deep in work. I remember when I finally found a baby sitter Isi and I could go to a movie together. Was I ever glad to get out! We saw Katherine Hepburn in *A Bill of Divorcement*. When we returned the sitter pointed to my framed college picture, taken a year ago and asked, "was that you?" I answered, "Yes." She sighed and said, "How beautiful you were." I was jolted. I realized how much my life and life style had changed.

I often think of that blistering hot July day in 1934. We were visiting Mama at her small house off the road, the first one she had bought and which she now used only in the summer. Here she had once catered to her boarders. It must have been 90 degrees or more in the shade. Not a leaf stirred. Not a breath of breeze. I had to heat the baby's bottle. Mama began to pile wood into her wood-burning stove. The temperature soared. Mama in her long petticoats did not complain. But I did. "Everyone in Chesterfield has electricity," I sputtered. "This is stupid!"

Mama succumbed. The generator days were over. She purchased and installed in the big house a stripped down electric stove, four burners and a small oven. It stood on four thin legs, cost $1.50 down and $1.50 a month for 18 months. I remembered the report I had written for my college economics class on the pros and cons of the Installment Purchase Plan that was being introduced to the country, on the premise it wouldn't succeed. In time Mama agreed to an artesian well, never again to worry about a drought and

The Transition

having to lug precious water from a spring in the woods. And, finally, she acquiesced to Butch, who presented her with an oil burner for the big house.

The first break I had in the daily routine of my life came when my mother consented to care for Mitchell, 18 months old, while Isi and I went to Florida on his vacation. I was thrilled. I loved the freedom, the change. Three days of travel by car through new places. After three days in Miami Isi decided to return. He was concerned about the baby. Thereafter, for several years any vacation we took our children accompanied us.

By 1935 Isi and I settled in Hartford. I enjoyed buying furniture and creating a home of our own even though it was an apartment. Anne, Butch's wife, took me under her wing. Their friends became ours too. I also had friends, though I, who had married at 21, was much younger than they. In the Depression many people waited until they could afford to marry.

And every Sunday, every holiday, national and religious, we spent at Mama's. It was a command performance.

In the early 1930's the rumble of Hitler's activity was increasing and became louder. I joined the American Jewish women's organization *Hadassah* (Hebrew for Esther) whose program was primarily medical social service work in Palestine, a land festering with disease. Hadassah also embraced the vision of Zionism, the establishment of a Jewish home on the ancient soil. In 1919 the English Balfour Declaration gave impetus to this idea and after World War I idealistic Jewish people began to trickle into Palestine, mostly from Eastern Europe. My mother had belonged to Hadassah when I was a child living in Norwich and I remember

I Remember Chesterfield

collecting money in a little blue and white box for the Jewish National Fund to purchase land there. When the president of the Hartford Chapter of Hadassah asked me to do a report on Current Events, I was elated. I felt I was back in school again, doing research and learning. This was the beginning of my long career in community volunteer activity. Isi encouraged me.

By October 1937, when our daughter Nancy was born, five years after my college graduation, my transition was complete. I had learned a great deal and was happy. I had The American Family, a boy and a girl, and a lovely apartment with a Steinway baby grand piano in the living room. I could play music again. I had my own car, live-in domestic help, a loving husband, intellectual stimulation, good friends. Hartford offered cultural events and we joined Tumblebrook Country Club. The only disquieting feature arose when Butch's successful business grew and his construction jobs were too distant for Isi to commute. Consequently he was often away from home.

Yet nothing disturbed the routine of Mama's family gatherings. For me Chesterfield was Mama, and Mama was Chesterfield. I did, however, now drive down to visit Aunt Helen or Uncle Jake on occasions, but the carefree halcyon days of my youthful Chesterfield experiences were over. They rest, treasured in my memory.

The Transition

Grandfather John Kaplan holding Nancy, 1938

Standing: Libby Solomon Krasnow. Seated: My mother, Ida Kaplan Solomon holding granddaughter Odette, and Ida's father John, holding his great-granddaughter Merle

My Grandfather
Chapter XV

My maternal grandfather, John Kaplan, often affectionately called by his Hebrew name, *Yayñah*, (Jonah), was born in 1866. I think of him, even in his advanced years, as a stalwart, commanding person. About six feet tall, he carried himself erect and with dignity. When he was young and slim and his dark hair matched his brown eyes he would have been handsome. In his oval face, always clean shaven, his features were regular. I admired his well-shaped nose. Once, when I watched him, dressed in a neat black suit, dance at a party, hands clasped behind his back, steps small and precise, I was surprised to note that for a large man, how light he was on his feet.

John was reputed to possess an impetuous and strong temper, but I never witnessed it. To me he was always kind, caring and, in retrospect, confiding. But when I consider his early years in Chesterfield, how he must have toiled single-handedly to eke out a meager living from his farm's limited acreage, he must have burst out in frustration many a time. What he endured would have challenged the patience of a saint. Yet, so many Jewish farmers in Chesterfield, also ill-equipped and agriculturally ignorant, suffered similar struggles.

Sometimes in retrospect, when I try to analyze John's life, I wonder to whom he could talk about his problems. His parents had died. His brothers were involved with their own families and struggles. Friends? I don't remember any. And Grandma, patient and burdened, had her own concerns. She would never criticize or cross

My Grandfather

him. Basically, I realize, he must have been alone and silent about his worries.

In winter Grandpa would go into the woods, hew trees, drag them back over the snow on the travois to the wood shed and chop them into manageable lengths. He carried in every stick of wood needed to provide heat, hot water and fuel for cooking. All the water drawn from the well, bucket by bucket, hand hauled by a rope, he brought in. When an outside pump was installed on the well the pump froze in zero weather and had to be primed with boiling water from Grandma's kettle. I still remember that.

Morning and evening, in blizzard or blistering summer heat, the cows were herded into the barn to be milked, the milk chilled and then taken by horse and wagon to the Creamery on Flanders Road, about a half mile away. Each day the barn had to be shoveled out, the hencoop cleaned, hay forked into mangers, the horse tended to, and in summer, an adequate garden planted.

The only break in this routine came on Saturday mornings and religious holidays when he joined the other Chesterfield Jewish people for worship in the little synagogue. Isi told me that John had a fine voice and when he and his three brothers, Yale, Max and Issac sang the religious passages a cappella, the music was extraordinary and inspiring. "Something to listen to," were Isi's emphatic words.

❦ ❦

Our first, fantastic trip to Italy Isi and I took in May 1962. We landed in Milan where I spied a poster displaying the famous Australian soprano, Joan Sutherland, who was going to sing at La Scala in

Lucia di Lammermoor. I wanted to go. Isi remarked how expensive the tickets were at $35.00 each, but we went.

It was a spectacular performance. I was elated at the privilege of hearing her. Never will I forget her last curtain call. She stood on the stage dressed in a somber dark green gown. Thrown from the orchestra and tiers of balconies, a cascade of flowers fell to her feet. Slowly she bent and selected a single deep red rose. Pressing it to her bodice, the tall, angular soprano gracefully bowed, acknowledging the thunderous applause and tribute the enthusiastic audience showered upon her. As we walked back to the hotel my mind raced to Chesterfield where Isi's and my humble roots lay. Here we were, having experienced the very essence of superb musical artistry, the epitome of phenomenal vocal talent, in a country, a city, my grandparents probably never knew existed. I said to Isi, "What do you suppose my grandfather would say if he saw us here tonight? This would be the farthest thing in his imagination."

"He'd be pleased," Isi answered me. "Your grandfather was very musical. You were too young to know that."

But, I thought, in all the years I had spent in Chesterfield, I never heard him sing, never burst into song with the joy of living, never heard him hum a tune.

By the time John was 31, the first four children born were girls, Rose, my mother Ida, Molly, Goldie; then Ben, Helen and Jake. Child labor among the Chesterfield Jewish farmers had to be common. My mother told me that when Aunt Rose was two years old

My Grandfather

she was sent to weed the garden. By the time she was six she drove the horse and wagon to New London to collect the summer boarders. I can imagine my grandfather, weary and hungry, walking into the kitchen crowded with seven small, noisy children. My grandmother would hand him a towel to wash up. If he were irritated or in a bad mood he might have cuffed the kids or even spanked them. "Spare the rod and spoil the child" was the accepted philosophy. However, all his children except Ben cared about and for him until his death.

After Rose and my mother were married in 1909, keeping boarders ceased for my grandparents. Without the girls to help Grandma couldn't manage. She had toiled long enough. Grandpa switched to renting rooms with cooking privileges to vacationing New York families. At the same time he must have built the store on his land facing the highway. Later he added the dance hall, which Uncle Jake managed. He still farmed, although he no longer depended on farming for income, maintaining a small herd of cattle and a garden. When Aunt Helen married in 1930 she assumed ownership of the store.

While Grandma lived, most of my Chesterfield experiences revolved around her. After she died Grandpa and I became closer.

When he remarried, soon after her death, his daughters were furious and told him so. I was the one to whom he spoke. "Micala," he explained plaintively, "every night when I would come home there was a light in the window to welcome me. The house was warm. Food on the table and Grandma was there. Now I can not walk into a

I Remember Chesterfield

cold, dark house (it was winter) and I will not live with any of my children."

I admired him for his independence and spirit. I could understand his predicament. Which daughter would he choose to spend the rest of his life with? Would they give him any peace? Would he be able to retain his identity? He realized he wouldn't.

According to Jewish law, a widow must wait three months before remarrying, so that should she be pregnant, the real father could be determined. But the little red-haired woman John was to marry was years beyond her childbearing years. Just the same, John and she had to wait the three months. When her time came and she died, Grandpa married again. By now the dance hall had been converted to apartments where they lived. After she passed away he moved into the Hebrew Home of the Aged in Hartford where I could see him more often. He died at the age of 78.

I always enjoyed Grandpa's visits. He knew I didn't maintain a strictly kosher kitchen, so he warned me. "Micala," he said to me one day, "don't tell me what I'm eating. It's more of a sin to insult your hostess by refusing to eat the food she serves you. But if I don't know what I'm eating I can't be accused of doing wrong. The sin isn't mine."

I wouldn't mind assuming such a trivial sin, however, deferring to my husband, I did observe some of the traditional laws. I purchased meat from a Jewish butcher, but I didn't soak it for an hour and then salt it for 30 minutes. I did not put butter on the table with meat. I did not use separate dishes, one for dairy products, one for meat related foods. On the other hand, I didn't bring forbidden foods into the house. But John was wary and made sure I understood how

My Grandfather

he felt. I figured his logic served him well and I would never offer him anything that was improper.

In 1943 Isi and I bought our first large home in West Hartford. I brought Grandpa to see it. When we came into the den where all my books were shelved he stopped, amazed. I can still see him standing there, awed. "Who reads all these books?" he demanded.

I don't know what he thought. Obviously he was impressed. He probably had never seen so many books together at one time. I answered him modestly and in a wee voice, "I've read most of them, Grandpa."

After he left I realized he never owned a book except the Bible and prayer books which were written in ancient Hebrew. He never had the pleasure of reading a lay book, one written in the Jewish text. I never saw any in the farmhouse. The letters of the Yiddish alphabet are the same as those of Hebrew, but Yiddish, based on a 12th century German vernacular, was spoken and read by the Jews living in the Russian Pale of Settlement. For a while it was lost as their descendants learned English, but currently Yiddish is enjoying a revival.

Grandpa delighted in his daily Jewish newspaper sent from New York. He relished the dramatic episodes of the serialized story. He mulled over the domestic problems, the crises, the solutions, the characters.

None of John's grandchildren had a Liberal Arts education except me. Several others reached higher degrees of vocational education, an accountant and successful investment broker, a pharmacist, social worker, teacher. My cousin Alfred became a lawyer and worked for the Government.

I Remember Chesterfield

What I admired most about Grandpa was his total acceptance of his life. He stayed in Chesterfield when so many other Chesterfield settlers, wooed by the Baron de Hirsch Fund, moved on, seeking more money or adventure. John worked hard and sought no favors. Fortunately he was physically strong. His pleasures were small and few, his relief seldom. Yet I never heard him bewail his fate. Nor did I ever hear him swear. He just did the best he knew how. His sister, great Aunt Esther, my own Aunt Rose and a few cousins were also gifted with this remarkable attribute of acceptance. They were down-to-earth people, comfortable, content and loveable.

I loved my grandfather well.

The night he died I had the most peculiar experience. I was home alone at our summer cottage on the waterfront at Attawan Beach, about 8 miles south of New London. I was very upset because David, my third child, 17 months old, lay ill with fever and listless in his crib. The rural doctor hadn't come for three days. I was beside myself with worry and I was stranded. I couldn't leave to take the baby back to Hartford to his pediatrician because that summer I had no car. Isi had gone into business for himself. Money was limited and he was using my car. Mitchell was off at camp and Nancy away visiting. I was uneasy, afraid, apprehensive. I felt something dire and foreboding was trying to come into the house. I sensed it. Like Death. When Isi phoned me, as he did every night, I begged him to drive down, even though it was 55 miles away. I did not want to be alone. He couldn't. I called my sister-in-law Bess who lived in New London and pleaded with her to come spend the night with me. "Something evil is here," I said. But she had one of her horrible migraine headaches and couldn't move. I was alone, trapped, and I, always

My Grandfather

calm in a crisis, was scared. Before I went to bed I pulled down every shade in the house, closed every door, even the bedroom one, brought David's crib close to my bed and spent a fearful night. "Whatever you are," I spoke into the darkness, "stay away from here." In every heightened sense of mine I felt its lurking presence.

Early the next morning Isi called me to tell me my grandfather had died the afternoon before. I knew then that the menacing unknown that threatened me had been the presence of death.

I Remember Chesterfield

The Jewish Agricultural and Industrial Society, c.1900
(Arrow indicates Jacob Savin)

Mama
Chapter XVI

I had first met Mama face to face that *Rosh Hashonah* day Isi brought me home to dinner. She stood in the dining room near the unlit brown heating stove, a tall, spare woman, leaning slightly to the left, a broken shoulder had not healed properly. Her thin gray hair was pulled straight back into a small bun. I noticed her skin carried an olive tone and was wrinkled, her nose large, her mouth sunken. But her gray eyes, barely discernible in small, unusual triangular slits fringed with black lashes and deep set above her high Slavic cheek bones, smiled at me. She was always hospitable. My grandmother had told me that when Mrs. Savin was young she was called double breasted, but on that day she was flat chested and no spare flesh clung to her lean body. Her plain housedress touched the floor.

She was very pleased to see me and welcomed me warmly. I was to learn what a most remarkable woman she was, what an exceptional mother-in-law she would become. Over the years I spent much time alone with her, listening to her, observing and appreciating her. I gleaned how astute and wise, ambitious and hard working, loyal, kind and devoted a person she was. She found no fault with her daughters-in-law, Anne, Edith and me. Admitting to herself the strong and complex personalities of her three sons, she warned them, "Good wives are hard to find."

Born in 1873 in Vitebsk Geburniya, White Russia, near the city of Dvinsk on the Dvina River, Sara Savin, nee Sonya Reitch, was the youngest of six children. Hennoch, her father, a well-to-do grain

I Remember Chesterfield

merchant, would sail down the river to buy crops and later sell them in Riga on the Baltic Sea. Mama was the only one of two people I ever heard sigh and say, "At home ..." and tell how wonderful life had been there, how happy she was, how marvelous were the fruits and vegetables.

When she was 18 years old, despite the Tsar's edict prohibiting emigration for Jews, Mama was wrested from her contentment and flung into the turmoil of escape. She fled with her married brother Wolf to America, a difficult and harrowing trip according to the various accounts told by his three daughters. There were no longer alternatives left to Wolf to escape being conscripted into the Russian army, a dreaded fate for religious Jewish men. Hennoch had already bribed all those officials who could be bought off. But why he sent his youngest daughter with Wolf and not one of his other older, unmarried children, or why Wolf didn't emigrate by himself as did thousands of other male émigrés, has always puzzled me. I can only rationalize that Sara was levelheaded, capable and possessed good judgement. He trusted her.

Hennoch must have also foreseen the future necessity of moving his family out of Russia. When they finally came to America, David, the oldest sibling remained. David was a Cantor whose voice, Mama said, was so powerful when he sang the very windows *trayselled* (rattled).

Wolf was discontent living in New York. When his family arrived he spurned the opportunity to purchase land in the Bronx. Rather, he bought a small place on Fire Street, in a poor rural district on the outskirts of New London, only a few miles from Chesterfield. Here Mama later joined them to help Mary, Wolf's wife, with their growing children. Mary came from an extremely wealthy family and brought with her trunks of expensive clothes, never worn by her in America and unfit for the role of an impoverished farmer's spouse. Mama, already an old maid at 23 and choosy, met and married Jacob Savin who was working in my great grandfather's pants factory in Chesterfield. From Jacob's picture I discern a man of medium height, dark hair and dark eyes. There is an intense look on his face.

My mother told me that Mrs. Savin's husband Jacob was very brilliant, very charming, but restless. "He didn't like living in Chesterfield and working on a farm. So he'd leave for New York where he found more excitement. Then he'd come back. She'd become pregnant. Again he'd leave for New York and when he returned she'd have another baby."

Of course there had to be much gossip and conjecture in Chesterfield about Jacob's irregular behavior which was contrary to the usual steadfast pattern of the Jewish settlers there. But knowing Mrs. Savin as I did, nobody learned anything more than what was common knowledge. My mother-in-law was a most private person and would never have disclosed or discussed her affairs or that which had transpired between her and her husband, with anybody except her brother Wolf, not even with her children.

She never spoke of Jacob to me. But I remember one day, after I'd been married several years and was staying alone with her on the farm, I found enough courage to say, "Tell me about Jacob. Of all your grandchildren only Bess's son is named for him." To perpetuate a family's given name among Eastern European Jewish people, a newborn child is named after the deceased person. Like Mitchell, named after my father.

I Remember Chesterfield

Mama was silent, gathering her thoughts. Then she said, "Three babies a year and a half apart. I wasn't going to be a brood cow, a baby every year, like the other women. I found out what to do." She sighed. "When I discovered I was pregnant with Isi I was upset. I hoped he'd be a girl." But I noticed she didn't mention Jacob.

About two years after Isi was born on June 10, 1909, Jacob died in New York. Just when and where he is buried none of Mama's offspring knows. It was her secret and she bore it in silence and dignity. I can only presume that the failure of her marriage – when she was utterly faithful – the embarrassment of Jacob's errant activities and his lack of support affected her profoundly. She cut his memory out of her life. He left her with four young children. Her parents lived with her. Hennoch, once so financially successful, now only taught Hebrew to the Jewish children in Chesterfield, not very lucrative. After Mama's sister Celia died she took in and cared for Celia's three young children until their father married again. On Mama's shoulders rested the responsibility and welfare of nine people. But she was already in business. She took in summer boarders, the pleasure folk.

Jacob, however, bequeathed to his children many of his characteristics. His restlessness and eagerness drove them to succeed. They inherited his charm and engaging personality. And his brilliance was evinced in their quick intelligence. From Mama they derived their perseverance and determination, their physical strength and their loyalty to each other.

In later years whenever the Savin family good-naturedly reminisced about the boarders there was much laughter. Bess had helped in the kitchen. Moe waited on tables. I remember how comical

Mama

Moe was when he imitated one of the older women in her broken English. "Pliss, Moey darhlink," she whines, "pliss, mine egg should be three and a half minnits, not three minnits, not four minnits, but pliss, Moey, be a gut boy, just three and a half minnits." We'd laugh. I could imagine Mama with her long petticoats in the summer kitchen trying to serve a six or seven course breakfast with variations to 30 or more guests and boiling, maybe three times, to get the egg just right, just three and a half minutes on an erratic wood-burning stove. She catered to everyone's whims.

When I married Isi, he said to me, "I washed and wiped so many dishes, I swept so many floors, I waited on tables, made so many beds. Washed blankets and sheets in the brook, I never want to do that again!"

To have a successful "season" for all those farmers who took in paying guests meant earning enough money during the summer to carry the family through the winter, a desperate necessity. How desperate I understood when Isi related to me the following story. "I had whooping cough one summer when I was nine years old. If the boarders got wind of that they'd flee with their kids and we'd lose the "season." So I roamed the woods with my dog during the day, and I'd sneak back into the house at night to eat and sleep."

The era of the boarders revealed the austerity, the tension, worry and unending struggle to survive that marked the early Jewish families in Chesterfield. My own mother, whenever she talked about her youth, was bitter. Bess, Isi's only sister, would emphatically recall

I Remember Chesterfield

Back Row: Mama, Moe, Honey Kirschenbaum, Bess Savin Kirschenbaum
Kneeling: Abe Kirschenbaum, son, Bobby Kaye

Mama

Back row: Butch, Isi. Seated: Herbert Savin, Mitchell, Mama holding Nancy, Peter Savin, 1938

the dread she felt that Mama would not be able to meet the mortgage payment. And Butch once remarked to me, "We were so poor I swore I'd never be poor when I grew up." He wasn't. His genius at business, his canniness, the fantastic financial success he achieved and the fortunes he accumulated are a legend. Mama always said, "Whatever Butch touched turned to gold."

Moe, if he only had had the financial means to pursue a legal career, would have been an outstanding attorney. He possessed a lightening comprehension and generously donated time and money to civic and religious affairs. In New London he served several terms as Mayor, was elected a Connecticut State Senator, and even ran for Congress, losing by only 1,000 votes. On the main campus of the

University of Connecticut the Hillel House carries his name because of his considerable efforts in its creation.

Despite Mama's straitened circumstances in the early days she would insist on assuming a positive attitude. "I tried to make our home *frailich*, joyful," she'd say. And she did. The table would be nicely set. There was good food and they sang. I remember how often, when all of us Savins were gathered around the extended table, should a lull in the noisy conversation occur, Bess would hop up, clap her hands and begin to sing a familiar, peppy Jewish melody we all could join. As if to inspire us with light heartedness. I always thought this gesture of hers was a leftover from the days when difficulties were so threatening. Then the Savin family would sing together, grateful for what they had, health, hope and each other.

Mama's Properties
Chapter XVII

In the Chesterfield community of which Mama was an intrinsic member she was highly regarded. She was admired for her strength, courage, intelligence, independence and most probably envied for her financially successful and prominent children.

She owned three farms, an accomplishment no other farmer in Chesterfield achieved. Her nearly 200 acres were never operated as income producing only, although after the heyday of boarders was over she maintained a small herd of cows and sold the milk to the New London Dairy. No longer did she plant a vegetable garden on the corner lot. Nor did she ever grow flowers outside. With the exception of a few begonia plants blooming in coffee cans no fresh flowers ever appeared. Occasionally she sold off a hay lot and Butch was allowed to make use of a gravel pit.

The first farm she bought with her husband Jacob was a most charming little Colonial house with 40 acres of land, "more or less" the deed states. It must have been built in the late 18th century. I can say that because on the day I visited the remarkable open air American museum in Shelbourne, Vermont, I walked into a dwelling that was the very exact duplicate of Mama's. It was dated either 1796 or 1798. I was thrilled to find it.

Halfway up a grassy slope in this "little farm" and parallel to the front door, which no one ever used, a low stone wall separated the house from the tree shaded bumpy lane I remember from my first ride with Isi. In the front entrance hall, no bigger than a scanty closet, a two foot wide staircase led up to a narrow catwalk off of which were tucked three gaily papered bedrooms with sloping ceilings and dormer windows. Mama had a penchant for large floral wallpaper patterns; she papered the rooms herself.

Downstairs, two good-sized attractive rooms, fireplaces boarded up, flanked the tiny hall. In back of these was the original kitchen with its well preserved wide floorboards, antique iron hinges and latches on the doors as well as many small square panes of glass in the windows. Along the inner wall a shallow fireplace rested on a miniature hearthstone, its itsy-bitsy Dutch oven built shoulder high. A borning room, big enough only to contain a bed and closet, another room remodeled as a bathroom and a large room Mama used as a kitchen when she lived there year round completed the layout.

Outside, off the driveway, which rose almost perpendicular from the bumpy lane, two stone steps with an imbedded iron mudscraper led to the side door entrance.

Across the driveway and facing the house stood a single story white building housing the summer kitchen and dining room, an upright piano in the far corner. Here Mama once coddled her summer boarders and later catered to her family during the summer.

The most wonderful thing about the "little farm" were the marvelous, rampant blueberry bushes growing in the meadows and further up the hill into the woods. There a magnificent oak tree stood offering a landmark so I would never be lost in my wanderings through the woods. At the end of Mama's property a huge glacial boulder towered. When Isi and I climbed it we beheld a spectacular view of the area. Often we would invite friends to blueberry picking

Mama's Properties

parties. Mama never washed the bloom off her blueberries. Rather, she culled them from the sticks and leaves while spread on a towel and then made fabulous pies. Thick cookie crusts with juicy berries oozing between.

I have no idea just when Mama bought her second farm of 60 acres. It faced the highway and was only a stone's throw from the "little farm." Here Mama had billeted additional boarders, but now lived in this "big house" during the winter months.

Previously Mama's dear friends the Schneiders had lived there until they moved to New London and established a hardware store. Then the Phillips family, also dear friends, occupied the dwelling until Mama purchased it. I didn't like the big house, one of the largest ones in Chesterfield. I thought it bare, grim and dark with a long empty front hall. Even though the architectural design of the house was comparable to my grandparents' there was a difference. In the front room where Grandma had her parlor, Mama stored her groceries; a 100 pound bag of sugar, the same of flour, onions, canned goods, rice, tea, coffee, eggs, her cooking utensils and other necessities. To fetch anything from here she walked from the sink room across the kitchen, through the dining room and her bedroom to retrieve perhaps an onion. Before an electric refrigerator was installed she had to go outside, down an irregular flight of stone steps into the cool cellar to select her perishables: butter, milk, root vegetables, carrots, potatoes and apples. She was endlessly walking.

Beyond minimum necessities, Mama was obviously not interested in furniture. However, a huge dining table dominated the dining room where Anne's discarded three piece living room set was placed against the outside wall. There were only beds and bureaus in each room of both houses. No mirrors, no pictures, no frivolities. Neither house had a pretty view. No orchard, no shady place to swing a hammock, no place to curl up and read a book. There was only a barren yard to park cars where the children played baseball with Moe, romped with their dog or rode their pony.

The third farm of 90 acres abutting Mama's "little farm" edged across the Salem line. Mama rented that house to Mrs. Wickson, a pleasant woman whom I met only once.

Despite the limited accommodations of Mama's properties, the freezing bedrooms during the Passover holidays, the single bathroom for so many people, the lack of bathing facilities, Mama's family came, week after week, year after year. There was plenty of space. No one scolded. And we, my wonderful sisters-in-law, had the rare opportunity to become inordinately fond and loyal to each other.

It was Mama's warm and devoted personality, her generous hospitality, the tacit commitment of her children and her agreeable daughters-in-law that brought us all together. Our children loved to go to Grandma's. They had superb times and as they grew older they retained fond affections and relationships with each other.

It was at Mama's house that I found a solid family.

Thanksgiving at Mama's

Chapter XVIII

My mother-in-law took great pride in her culinary prowess. After all, she had maintained a successful summer business. The same boarders returned year after year, content in their choice of a vacation hotel.

I realized, however, Mama was not the same sort of cook as my grandmother. Though they chose the same kinds of ingredients their final results were different. My people had immigrated from Belarus, White Russia. Mama came from Latvia, closer to Riga and Germany. They even displayed dissimilar pronunciation for the same foods. Aunt Helen said *keegal*, Mama said *kugel*. Aunt Helen said *pitter*, Mama said *putter* (butter). Because I had picked up a spotty and limited vocabulary from Mama — my family never spoke Yiddish to me — I could use a meager Yiddish dialect as she did, always feeling disloyal to my forefathers.

My grandmother preferred dairy, fish and fresh farm products. Mama chose meats, starchy foods and leaned heavily on sugar and fats. Seldom did butter, cream, cheese or much milk appear on Mama's menu. Nor did she ever make borscht, gefilte fish or farmer's cheese. My grandmother opted for rendered chicken fat (high class). Mama would purchase 20 pounds of good beef suet from her butcher and render it. All her cooked foods were either fried or baked in it. When the vegetable shortening NYAFAT came on the market she switched to that.

I Remember Chesterfield

But Mama prepared three outstanding dishes I cannot duplicate. She made a toothsome carrot *tsimmes*. After boiling unpeeled carrots until soft she'd slip off the skins, neatly slice them in thin circles, add a mixture of water, sugar, flour and with or without a piece of meat, and place it all in a shallow casserole. Sometimes, but not often, she'd include potatoes. In a slow oven it baked until the water had thickened and the *tsimmes* was a delectable pudding to be served as an accompaniment to the main course.

I remember her fabulous veal cutlets were an epicurean delight. All of us relished them and usually fancied them first. Dipping each cutlet in beaten egg, then flour, she sautéed them in a generous amount of fat until they were juicy and tender under a thick, tasty crust.

She seldom made her luscious rice pudding but I remember how much I enjoyed it. First, in the top of a double boiler she steamed the rice in milk until it was soft. Then she added sweet cream, eggs, raisins, sugar and cinnamon, poured it into a low pan and baked the pudding until it was browned, rich and delicious.

But on Thanksgiving Mama rolled out an array of her best dishes. No Pilgrim could have ever imagined such a feast!

On that day Mama's immediate family, all 17 of us, plus a few stranded Connecticut College students and lonely guests arrived at the big house sometime after noon. Quickly we piled out of our cars, bounded up the wide stone steps, burst through the door. Calling greetings, we threw our coats on the bed in the next room and made a beeline to the potato pancakes stacked in the warming oven of her wood-burning stove. These were not brown, dainty and crisp. Rather, they were huge, greenish, thick and hefty, guaranteed to stave off

Thanksgiving At Mama's

hunger. Mama peeled the potatoes three days previously and kept them in cold water until she grated them early Thanksgiving morning and fried them. We devoured them plain, no applesauce, no sour cream.

My task each holiday, which I enjoyed doing, was to create the centerpiece. In the oversized stemmed black glass bowl that I had purchased I piled oranges, rosy apples, bananas and pears, tucked in dried figs, apricots and walnuts, then draped it all with small clusters of black and green grapes.

By 1 o'clock everyone had appeared. We sat down at the table, extended by five boards, which Bess had set with snow-white linen cloth, polished silverware, matched plates, silver wine goblets and glasses for soda water. In the one hushed moment of the afternoon Bess's husband Abe offered the Thanksgiving prayer. Thanks to God for His gifts, our togetherness, good health, good fortune, our freedom, our wonderful country.

Then the noise began. Everyone talked simultaneously. Everyone had something to say, an opinion, a contrary view. No one spoke softly. There was a wonderful feeling of exhilaration, fellowship and affection. We laughed a lot.

From a seemingly bottomless pot Mama served her appetizer, small finger shaped rolls of ground meat rolled in cabbage leaves and simmered in a sumptuous tomato and raisin sauce. These were painstaking and time consuming to prepare. But how yummy.

Clear chicken soup followed with an accompanying platter of *kreplach*, triangular shaped pieces of dough like ravioli stuffed with chopped meat and baked until the edges curled crisp and browned.

A big turkey, stuffing and gravy.

I Remember Chesterfield

Mama carried in a special treat, not often made, a casserole of prunes and thickly sliced white potatoes. A bowl heaped with her delectable *tsimmes* and a platter of noodle pudding cut in squares. Like my grandmother, Mama made her own noodles. Rolling out a thin dough, she draped it on a muslin towel over the back of a chair to dry until it was ready to slice. Her *kugel* was not embellished with fruit like Grandma's. Hers was comprised of noodles, eggs and fat. I didn't eat it.

"Every Thanksgiving dinner has to have a sweet potato casserole," Edith, Moe's wife, insisted. Hers came to the table, marshmallows melting on top.

Store bought canned peas, a delicacy, no salad, Mama was not fond of greens, but celery and olives, Ocean Spray cranberry sauce and Mama's ambrosial, rosy, cold applesauce. Boiling water and sugar until syrupy, she added chunks of apples, sometimes peeled, sometimes not, which slowly simmered until soft but retained their shape.

I once asked Mama why we didn't have squash. "Squash?" She didn't know about that. "Turnips? They're for cows," she dismissed them with a disdainful wave of her hand.

Her idea of serving was to present every portion of food on a separate plate for each individual. She had a multitude of dishes, remnants from the boarders' era.

We feasted like starving Armenians.

When no one wanted or couldn't eat any more we women cleared the table. The men settled down to listen to the ball game on the radio. The children dashed outside to play. In the miniature sink

Thanksgiving At Mama's

room Mama washed the mountain of dishes with hot water from the tank on the side of the stove and we dried them.

In the waning light of the afternoon Edith and I would go for a walk. We'd cross the main highway and stroll down the narrow lane, past the little house, the frost tinged meadows, the shorn fields, the line of leafless trees. Usually the day was nippy and clear. We always had so much to talk about. Our marriages both happened in 1932. Our children were of comparable age. Both of us were involved in community affairs and we could always chat about the other members of the family. When darkness became imminent we'd saunter back to the house. The ball game was over. The children piled in and Mama served tea.

Just strong tea. No lemon. No cream. Everyone was hungry for the desserts. The table seemed to groan again. I had baked a chocolate cake and brownies. Edith brought her lemon sponge cake. But Mama's variety of delicious pastries was the most popular. Two generous apple pies, their plump cookie crusts enveloping a layer of cinnamon sugared apples. Trays of strudel puffed with filling of fruits and nuts. Bowls of her fantastic strawberry preserves, which she had made last June. Measuring two cups of sugar to two cups of firm whole strawberries, she let them stand overnight. In the morning she drained the juice and simmered it until it became syrupy. Careful not to break any berry, she added each one whole, cooking them gently for about 15 minutes or so until they became limp but retained their shape. Then she poured the mixture into quart jars and screwed the lids on tight.

Highlights of the afternoon were two of her outstanding specialties. Purchasing the largest prunes available, each one about three inches big, she stuffed them with blanched almonds and slowly stewed them in a sugared syrup. Not one prune broke open. Big, black, beautiful and yummy, Mama served them in a white bowl. And her *taglach* were superb! I've never tasted any other as good. Small balls of dough leisurely cooked in gingered honey and carefully watched until they became gooey, sticky and fit for the Gods. These tidbits demanded hours of preparation and constant vigilance. When we raved about these wondrous *taglach* Mama's closed smile reflected how much she had enjoyed rolling the tiny balls in her workworn hands and never cared how long she stood at the stove stirring the honey because she anticipated our pleasure. Not a *taglach* was left!

In short order all the sweets were eaten. The fruit disappeared, the boxes of candy were depleted. Now content and well fed, we were ready to drive home. Night settled in. Bundled up against the raw cold, we left one family at a time. Mama stood near the door and handed each one of her daughters-in-law a good sized Care Package including her fragrant cinnamon-raisin coffeecake buns. No doubt she was eminently pleased with the success of the day. In Yiddish she wished all of us *"Iber a yore, nuchk a mol."* "Next year, once again."

We looked forward to that.

Mama and I
Chapter XIX

As I sit and write about Mama and Chesterfield on a gloomy, morose winter day the memory of another such time surfaces.

It is January 1925, a similar, dismal, cold afternoon. Just home from the Academy, I have walked into the living room of our new home and can see the blur of my father as he rests in the shadows. He talks to me but I don't remember exactly what he says. But the grave tone of his voice has lingered all these years and I understood what his message to me was meant to be.

I always endeavored to live up to my father's hopes. It never crossed by mind to indulge in sex, drugs or alcohol. I possessed too much self-pride. I promised myself I'd be strong and responsible. When I was 55 and sought psychiatric help for an unrelated problem, my psychiatrist, Dr. Weisel, said to me, "You tried to wear your father's shoes." He was right. And my mother, from the time I was 14 years old, evidently trusted me. She gave me much freedom, asked no questions, offered no advice. Consequently, whenever I needed to know or do something I had to ferret it out myself. I had no role model, no one of experience to ask, no one to guide me in my decisions.

In retrospect I think this was why I admired my mother-in-law so much. In the 20 years after I married Isi I frequently spent much time alone with her. I realize how comparable she was to my father. He was born in 1880, she in 1873. Both emigrated from the approximate location in Russia, near the Baltic Sea. They possessed the same kind of dignity, humility, pride, patience and wisdom. I particularly respected the brilliant, controlled manner with which Mama treated people, especially her family. In many respects Mama became my role model. By example she illustrated what I deemed important and worthwhile.

I remember one time, probably during the Depression, Moe, her oldest son, had run into some financial difficulty. Mama was terribly upset. To be sure, she would never tell me or discuss the problem with me, but as I observed her I could see how perturbed she was. She paced, endlessly, back and forth, back and forth, carrying out her daily tasks. And she sang, the only time I ever heard her sing like that. Her voice was clear and full toned. I was surprised. And the haunting melody of Franz Schubert's *Serenade*, which she repeated over and over, echoed her anguish, her heartache.

Yet, when Sunday rolled around and her family came as usual for dinner, she treated us like royal guests. The underlying tension was there but suppressed. She asked no questions, did not express her fears, nor did she reproach anyone. There was no discussion. Nothing was mentioned. "The show went on."

Mama had probably already placed the dilemma in the good Lord's hands. She strongly believed in Him, the One Above who had decreed her fate. She relied on Butch, her strongest son, whose loyalty and business acumen would find the answers. Which he did. He was always supportive of the family, especially in a crisis.

Mama and I

❧❧

In my memory I have a clear picture of Mama on one of those indescribably exhilarating New England Spring days. I stand in the dining room watching her as she returned from the barn where she had been milking. Clad in a light jacket, full skirts and felt boots, she slowly walked up the huge stone slab steps to the house. Turning, she paused. Framed in the open doorway she gazed out beyond the barren yard to the distant meadows pale green with young grass, the unclouded sky. In the cool damp air of early morning hung the faint scent of fertile soil stirring, the nascent promise of new beginnings and rebirth. For a long time she was silent. Then, as she entered the house, she said to me, "I could never live in the city."

❧❧

As I think back I realize what an insular and isolated life Mama carved out for herself. Her mother died in 1932, her father long before that. She preferred to live alone on her property with only Major, a handy man to help her.

In a separate part of the big house, with a separate entrance, Major, a gentle old sot, had his quarters. As long as Mama poured him a generous slug of whiskey in his breakfast coffee he was content to hobble around doing odd jobs. In the fall he'd gather apples, take them to the cider mill and come home with a barrel of cider. As it grew harder he was happier. During Prohibition Mama

I Remember Chesterfield

would buy him the hair dressing Bay Rum which he drank. It contained 40% alcohol. During the week Major was the only person she saw.

I remember an incident that shook me profoundly. One Labor Day after everyone who'd summered with Mama had gone home I stayed on for a few days. Together we enjoyed the beautiful September weather in the country, the peace, the unaccustomed quiet. We had no radio in the little house. We read no newspapers. The telephone was across the road in the big house. We were unaware of the world beyond Chesterfield. Just sufficient and content with ourselves.

When Isi returned on Friday night he informed us that Senator Huey Long had been assassinated. I was appalled! To think how cut off I had been, how far removed from the throbbing pulse of current history. But it had no significance for Mama. She would read about it later. She had chosen to live within a circumference she could manage. She never complained, never bewailed her fate, never said she was lonely. Her solitary meals, her daily monotonous chores, the long winter nights …

Whenever Mama had company she was relaxed and charming. She could converse intelligently with the business guests Butch invited home. But none of her contemporary farmers' wives came to call. Too far for them to walk to her house. Nor did she visit them. Mama was sorry she didn't learn to drive a car. In 1952, nearly 80, she had the courage to fly in Butch's private plane to Binghamton, New York to attend his son Pete's wedding. I think of Mama as a survivor, victorious after each accomplishment. A meal well cooked and served, a day's labor finished, an incident concluded, a vexing problem solved. Victories all.

❦ ❦

I remember the first trip to Paris that Isi and I took. We walked into the Louvre on a lovely May morning. At the end of a long room I spied the Nike of Samothrace, The Winged Victory, mounted high on a dais dominating the space. Symbol of an ancient Greek military victory. With awe I admired its grace and exquisite proportions and I thought all victories are not so grandly memorialized. Every Russian Jewish farmer's family in Chesterfield who fought each day to survive, like Mama, had their triumphs.

How could we be in Paris and not go to its famous Flea Market? Isi was unusual. He loved to go shopping. I remember the fun we had wandering around in the open air. A painting caught my eye. In its antique, old wooden frame something about its intense green foreground, the slope of the light horizon, the sky and feeling of open space reminded me of Grandpa's farm. It seemed to be of the Impressionist period but the signature was blurred. We bought it.

I was so pleased when I showed it to my mother and she said, "Looks like Grandpa's farm."

❦ ❦

Mama was deeply religious in her heart and believed in God's will. She observed all the religious restrictions concerning dietary laws but wasn't above skirting a rule or two. One Passover when David, our younger son, was two or three, we were staying the whole eight days with Mama at the big house. David would not eat any of the Passover foods. He wanted his familiar spaghetti. Thanks to her accommodating nature Mama handed me an old pan, plate and fork and let me boil his food on the electric stove and wash the utensils in the bathroom. These activities occurred in spite of the dismay and angry vocal criticism of my brother-in-law Abe with whom she never argued. David survived. So did Abe.

Like other Jewish wives in Chesterfield, Mama kept a kosher kitchen. They didn't know anything else. Two sets of dishes, one for meat products, one for dairy foods. Two sets of silverware. Two sets of pots and pans. The kosher meat she purchased she soaked for an hour, then salted it for 30 minutes according to Judaic law. During Passover all the cooking utensils and serving dishes had to be changed. The stored Passover necessities came up from the cellar. All leftover daily food was destroyed or packed away until the holiday was over.

Mama had a droll sense of humor. Aunt Doris came to visit me one afternoon. When she was about to leave and Mama stood close by, she asked Mama, "Mrs. Savin, will you sell me a quart of milk?"

"No," Mama answered.

Doris and I were startled. This was not like Mama, who then smiled and said, "I'll give it to you."

Mama and I

⚜⚜

I must commend her for her perseverance, her extraordinary physical energy, her lofty ambitions. Her daily tasks demanded her time but she was not intellectually diminished. She was keenly aware of politics and politicians. I often marveled at her poise and wisdom, she who had spent most of her life owning and working on a humble farm.

⚜⚜

In 1953 Mama closed her big house and moved to New London to live with her daughter Bess. She was the last of the original Russian farmers to leave. Already gone were the Cohens, Schwartzs, Kayes, Millers, Leviloffs and Kaplan families, the ones I knew. And gone for me were the huge Sunday dinners, the religious holidays spent in Chesterfield. I loved my sisters-in-law, admired their husbands and liked being with them. It was the monotony I chafed at. Now, at last, each of us women could create her own traditions. Our holidays became truly joyful. Our house filled with flowers and good wishes from family and friends. And it shone, as Mama would say, from end to end.

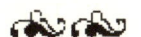

⚜⚜

Much as I respected, admired and esteemed my mother-in-law, I didn't love her. She wasn't loveable. I well acknowledge the many times when Isi was away I drove down to her farm in Chesterfield because I felt comfortable and wanted there, but I could never bring myself to hug her or say, "I love you." A resolute woman, she always stood a few steps away from a person, even if she were smiling.

Nor was Mama attractive. She used no creams or cosmetics. Her work-worn fingers were swollen and arthritic. She didn't avail herself of any beauty parlor treatments. She just wasn't pretty. When she dressed for a party she was enhanced by the handsome dresses Anna bought for her.

I could never doubt her loyalty and fierce love for her children; her grandchildren were so precious to her they carried an aura of holiness. Yet she was not affectionate. I never heard her scold, reprimand or punish any of them, they had free run of any situation, but I never saw her pick up, cuddle or kiss one either. Nor did she spend any time alone with a grandchild. She was not affectionate. Isi once told me his mother never kissed him.

Nor was she articulate. Mama never expressed her feelings. I never heard her say, "I'm sorry," or "I'm sad," "It pleases me," or "I'm angry." I never heard her lose her temper or raise her voice. She never bared her heart. She didn't gossip. The one emotion she considered evil and destructive was jealousy.

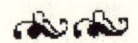

Mama and I

Good and generous as Mama was to me and my children, I harbored a suppressed resentment. As Isi's wife I was an intrinsic part of her family but never a part of the inner circle of Butch, Mama and Bess. I was silently annoyed with Mama's pull on my husband's love, his utter devotion to her and his deference to her wishes. I would never interfere, never openly criticize and never insist he choose between us. I knew I wouldn't win nor did I ever want to disparage his opinion of his mother, although I knew she was wrong.

For years Mama nursed a dream that her three sons would unite in a single business venture. To her, as she often reiterated, a doctor was a dirty job, a lawyer was a crook; a businessman was the best. Each of her three sons was too independent, too individual to bond together and cede to her aspirations for them. Until each son was well established, Mama never stopped trying.

※ ※

In 1962 Mama developed colon cancer. "I have the good thing," she said to Bess. There was talk of an operation. "Cancer grows slowly in older people," the doctor said.

Nobody consulted me. I didn't expect it. "She's going to die anyhow," I discussed the situation with Edith. "If she dies on the operating table she'd be spared a horrible and painful death." Edith didn't agree with me.

But, could Mama stand the trauma of an operation, she who had never suffered a sick day in her life? There was no operation. She took to her bed and whenever her pain was intolerable Bess went downstairs to sterilize a needle for a merciful shot of morphine.

I Remember Chesterfield

A few days before she died, Isi and I were in New London to visit her. When we walked into her bedroom I was surprised to note a history book on her night table which she must have been reading in her better moments.

"Look Mama," I said as I thrust my wrist close to her. "Look at the lovely gold bracelet Isi bought me for our anniversary."

Slowly she raised her head a little bit and with her drug dazed eyes peered closely at the bracelet. Then she lay back and asked me, "Where are the diamonds?"

Mama died early in July 1963. She was 90 years old.

At her funeral the Rabbi recited in Hebrew the one Psalm devoted to women. "A woman of valor who can find, for her price is far above rubies." But Mama, I thought, was smarter than the legendary, industrious Biblical heroine.

With her death, that which had been her Chesterfield for me was gone. Once I married Isi, Chesterfield was Mama. The only people left for me were Aunt Helen and Uncle Sam whom I stopped to see whenever I passed through the village.

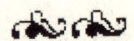

Mama and I

The Savin family, Lighthouse Inn, 1951

After the family dinners in Chesterfield ceased in 1953 Bess, whose birthday fell on December 25, and Abe would host an annual extended family party at Lighthouse Inn in New London. At least 60 people would gather to enjoy themselves. In time tragedy and death claimed its toll. Nancy, David and I held the last party of Mama's descendants and spouses several years ago. As the family dispersed in different directions the rifts in physical contacts deepened, although loyalty to the memory of the original Savin family stayed strong.

Today, as I look back and consider Mama's descendants, I wonder how she would presently regard them. I had perceived a dominant and altruistic sense of loyalty among her four children and her. All for one and one for all. Mama would say, "You have to help others. You must submit yourself for them." I always thought that behind this moving force of hers she naturally wanted her family to stay together. And they did. But I believe she must have needed to justify and ennoble herself because her actions determined her difficult life. When she escaped from Russia with her brother Wolf she sacrificed all she cherished. Nothing in America equaled what she had forfeited. So loyalty to her family reigned supreme. Over other emotions as love and affection of which I observed few or no expressions I often heard, "Help each other." This included her nieces and nephews.

Among Mama's nine grandchildren there were four divorces. Mama would have been horrified. And of her 21 great grandchildren 11 married non Jewish people. Mama would have been crushed. Yet, despite the prevalence of divorce today, all the marriages of her great grandchildren are solid and exemplary.

If Mama could witness her descendants she would have to be eminently proud. She had concentrated on accumulating wealth because, like the Chesterfield Jewish farmers, she was poor. Today, her third and fourth generation offspring all have higher degrees of education from the finest colleges in the country with two law degrees and several PhD's in history, astrophysics, and pyschology. All are financially successful and some are very well-to-do.

It is interesting and satisfying for me to note that the same traits Mama exemplified still flourish and are evident. Mama's individualism, independence, physical strength, ambition, hard work and charitable altruism are obvious characteristics among her over 40 descendants.

Mama and I

In the 100 plus years since Mama lived in the simple little early Colonial farmhouse on the bumpy lane, as yet unpaved, a staunch American family has emerged. Mama's spirit still lives.

I Remember Chesterfield

Isadore Savin

I Find My Russian Roots
Chapter XX

For years Isi and I, steeped in the customs and beliefs of the Russian Jewish immigrants who settled in Chesterfield, had talked about, dreamed about visiting the Soviet Union. His parents, my maternal grandparents and my father had been born in Russia and I was only one generation away. Our interest was great. Yes, there had been dramatic changes in Russia since the late nineteenth century, but much might have remained the same. We wondered how it would be to walk the very earth, to breathe the air, to see typical faces of our childhood, to taste familiar foods we once enjoyed. Finally, in 1972, the Soviets, relaxing some of their Iron Curtain policies, were accepting certain foreign travelers. Isi was so excited when I signed us up to join a Trinity College Soviet tour in August. So was I. We began to count the days.

※ ※

Isi died suddenly on Monday, June 19, 1972. Two days later, on our 40th anniversary, the children and I laid him to rest. He was only 63 years old.

How well I remember the previous Sunday night. We had attended a wedding where he danced his fool head off. Gifted with a wonderful sense of rhythm and a natural ear for music, he always threw himself into the spirited dances he remembered from his early Chesterfield days whenever the Jewish farmers gathered for a festivity. He was too young to have attended Grandpa's Dance Hall. Not for him were the popular Cha-Cha, Rumba or Mexican Hat Dance. The Israeli Hora, the circle dance, was his favorite when the tempo of the music whirled faster, faster, faster until the dancers, breathless, practically collapsed. That Sunday night he had a fantastic time.

The next morning he had risen early, "Don't get up," he said as he kissed me goodbye. "I'll have breakfast downtown."

He never came home again. He died in the doctor's office that afternoon. With him perished my most intimate, most precious bonds to Chesterfield.

I was dazed, devastated, destroyed. My beautiful, comfortable world shattered. I felt his death rejected me. I realized I had needed him more than the air I breathed, the food I ate. Without him I had no meaning, no identity, so aptly portrayed on that *Rosh Hashonah* holiday the following September. Instead of florists delivering bouquets of flowers for the holidays, good wishes from friends and family, no one sent me anything. All I found on my front door step that holiday eve was a single, lonely, dried up oak leaf the wind had blown in.

How well I remember that summer of mourning, how slowly the hours crept, like crippled centipedes, as I wept and wrote countless thank you notes. When evening approached and I expected Isi to come home I fled the house – to anywhere. The dark nights I couldn't face alone I slept at Anne and Butch's house, waking at dawn to sneak out quietly. Weekends I escaped to New London where Bess and Abe's saddened hearts embraced and comforted me. It took me seven months before I had the courage to turn over in my bed and confront that empty pillow. Life would never be the same without him.

For the next two years a broad, black band stretches across my memory, except for three major, catastrophic incidents.

In December 1972, a crushing ice storm caused thousands of dollars damage to the magnificent new home Isi had recently built, even indulging me with a large indoor swimming pool. Now I was forced to manage the repairs myself. I wept.

In the following summer, 1973, I sold our beach home. Never again would I enjoy my morning coffee on the wide front porch overlooking the sun's sparkling diamonds on the blue waters of Niantic Bay, seagulls swirling in a cloudless sky, a gentle east breeze caressing me. I would never again dabble my toes in the hushed lapping of the little waves as they washed against the pebbly shore. Never again would I stroll the curve of the beach searching for remnants of sea-washed glass. Nor would I wait for him in the evening twilight when the last rays of the setting sun lingered on the old pear tree and pink clouds floated in the sky. And I would never fall asleep again in his arms to the cadence of the sea below my open window.

I felt as though I sold my soul.

Soon after Isi died I sold Mama's little house with an acre of land, to a young couple who fell in love with its antiquities. Never again would I go blueberrying in the meadows and woods, although I retained the remaining acres.

My mother died in October 1973. A sudden, swift, fatal heart attack. I did not cry. I had no tears left. I couldn't bear to scatter her ashes to the wind with nothing to remember her by. I took them and buried them in our family plot.

Slowly I fought my way back to the land of the living.

※ ※

I never relinquished our dream of going to Russia. In February 1976, four years after Isi died, my travel agent tacked me on to a tour of a compatible Deerfield Academy Alumni group visiting Moscow, Kiev, Odessa and Leningrad, under the leadership of Michael Sanin who taught Russian at the school. His parents and grandparents had escaped the Soviets long before. It promised to be a wonderful trip.

I didn't know anyone in the group but I wasn't afraid to travel as a single person. I knew I wouldn't wander away to search out anything about my ancestors. I had no knowledge of exactly where they lived. No one ever mentioned names. Nor did I want to be arrested and languish in some Soviet prison. Just to be in the land of my people would be an experience!

"I wouldn't give those Commies a nickel of my money," my brother-in-law Abe scolded me when I informed the Savin family of my impending journey.

I didn't care. I shrugged off his comments. The mystery of Mother Russia, my love for the passionate music of the Russian composers, the Russian authors whose dramatic literature I had enjoyed had long intrigued me. I wanted to taste, feel, and see what Russia had been like for my people. My strong desire overcame the contempt I held for the Communist regime.

I Find my Russian Roots

Several hours after we flew from New York our plane landed at Sheranetyevo, Moscow's International Airport. Tired, exhilarated, eager, I handed my passport to the customs official, a serious faced, full breasted woman whose hair was dyed a peculiar shade of purple-red, a color I had not seen in any other country.

"Groupa?" she asked.

I smiled and answered, "Groupa."

She stamped my passport and I was in the USSR — Hurrah!

During the long ride toward the city I was amazed by the well-maintained two-lane road cleared of snow. However, I saw no other traffic either coming or going. Gazing overhead at the lighting I chuckled. Single bulbs screwed into single sockets on a wire looped from pole to pole. Mile after mile. Ingenious, primitive, not esthetic but serviceable. And for a long stretch on the right hand side of the highway more than a hundred small houses in a single row, alike as cookies squeezed out of a cookie press, bordered the road. A narrow porch, two windows downstairs, one on the second floor and a sharply peaked roof reminded me of childrens' party hats. The houses did not look occupied. No smoke out of the chimneys. No visible signs of life. No means of transportation.

As we rode into the city in the early dark I observed the shoddy, shabby, neglected box-like apartment houses the Soviets had built. I thought of my grandfather's property in Chesterfield. His buildings were shabby too. Not trim and tidy, unpainted.

I Remember Chesterfield

I shall never forget my first stunning, fascinating impression of Red Square that night. Emerging from the underground tunnel I stood at the entrance. I could not have imagined that the Square stretched so vast, so enormous, so bleak and cold. A sudden, swift blast of Arctic air sweeping down from the top of the planet across the frozen tundra with nothing in its path to impede its fury, tore at me, flung open my belted coat, battered my knees as I struggled to stand upright. My God! I thought. Ahead of me at the far end I beheld with awe St. Basil's Cathedral. Brilliantly illuminated, nine different sized circular turrets capped with onion domes, magnificently designed and elaborately decorated in glorious shades of rose and midnight blue, green and gold, adorned with flowers and spirals, shone. A gorgeous Oriental fantasy. Later I was horrified to learn that Tsar Ivan the Terrible had blinded the Italian architects so that never again would they be able to create another such extravagance.

High on the Kremlin roof glowed the ruby red symbol of the Soviet Union, proclaiming their power. The Soviet flag, hammer and sickle, danced madly in the violent wind. I joined the thin line of solemn people inching toward Lenin's tomb that was flanked by an honor guard of two soldiers. From a distance I thought they had to be statues, so rigid and frozen were the figures. But, coming closer, when I saw their reddened noses, I realized the men were real. At 9 o'clock bells tolled and the relief guard, two other handsome, strapping soldiers, goose-stepped forward. I hoped they were well fortified with vodka.

The searing, unremitting cold was unbearable. I stepped out of line. I really didn't care about peeking through the glass of Lenin's

I Find my Russian Roots

tomb. I hurried back to the Intourist Hotel to my small, barren, mediocre room.

When I opened my suitcase for my nightgown I saw that the Soviet police had already gone through my clothes and possessions. Miffed slightly, I pulled down the gray coverlet of my single cot and immediately was exultant. The same kind of big square feather pillow that Grandma possessed, the same inches-high down quilt. As I slid beneath it my memory raced back to Chesterfield on cold winter nights when my college friend Saul drove me to Grandma's after a date. The yellow light in the warm kitchen, the flannel nightgown she handed me. I fell asleep wrapped in her love once more.

I wasn't wildly impressed with Kiev after spending six long tedious hours in its airport waiting for the plane coming from Siberia. At 4AM we groggily climbed aboard the darkened plane, groped for seats and two hours later landed at Odessa. The men who guided the plane as it taxied in looked like upright polar bears, so swathed in furs were they. Only the tiny slits revealed their anxious eyes. And it was cold! It felt like 50 degrees below zero. As though the North Pole had swung down and usurped Odessa. The very air hung immobile, frozen, noiseless, strange.

I remember the long drive to the hotel in the predawn dark. I saw nothing move. Nothing stirred. No human walked the bleak sidewalks. No cat prowled. No paper fluttered. Even the convoluted branches of the naked, stunted trees curled in frigid discomfort. Was this the kind of land my people had lived in?

We passed miles of three story apartment houses. In the top sections of many lighted windows I could see a single electric light bulb screwed directly into the ceiling. On the stark white walls I saw no pictures, no plants, no decorations, no person. A plain white curtain, probably strung on a cord, obscured the lower half of most windows. I thought of Mama whose farm houses were so meagerly furnished.

Despite the smiling face of the maid as she welcomed us, the aged hotel was brown, dingy and grim. The heavy rugs thick with dust. Walking into my room I noticed the high ceiling in the bathroom was wet, stained and flaking; the damn gooseneck plumbing disgusted me. Against the cruel cold the radiators hissed bravely, but the air was icy. I threw my fur coat on the bed and as quickly as I could snuggled under the glacial sheets wondering, "How do people live in this kind of weather?"

I thought of my father's family and Mama who had lived several hundred miles further north. They had survived for centuries. From the Baltic to the Black Sea my people had endured this inhuman weather. They had to be strong, courageous and determined, exactly like the people I was familiar with in Chesterfield. I began to understand the hard-edged bareness of their lives. Flowers, pictures decorating walls, beautifully furnished rooms simply had no value against the daily needs of survival.

I didn't see much of Odessa, an important naval and shipping port on the Black Sea, and once a renown music center. I shunned the city tour to search for a piece of fresh fruit. Sam, who had spent a college year in Finland and spoke Russian well, accompanied me. Into small store after small store we walked. Into ugly restaurants where the food was dismal brown and slathered with fat, even into a cafeteria where the pale green paint was peeling off the walls. There was no fresh or canned fruit to be found. Only pickled foods and unattractive cold meats generously larded with slabs of suet. Obviously, the Soviets imported nothing they didn't grow themselves. People lived off their native produce. Finally I found an orange in the bar of a hotel and paid 50 cents for it.

I thought of Grandma and Mama, the winter vegetables they served were the same as we were being given: potatoes, carrots, beets, cabbage, dilled cucumbers and green tomatoes preserved in brine. Fruits were dried: raisins and apples, compotes of stewed dried prunes and pears. Mama canned jars of peaches and both women made an assortment of jellies.

Out of the left window of the plane I saw the pale blue Bay of Finland rise; the Neva River a black streak in the jagged ice; a multitude of roof tops and smoking chimneys; frozen little canals under petite bridges; and then we landed at St. Petersburg. I was utterly thrilled, choked with emotion and expectation. Had any of my ancestors ever been here?

St. Petersburg, Leningrad during the Soviet era, turned out to be the most elegant of the four cities our tour visited, the most disturbing for me, the most exhilarating. As we made our way to the Europa Hotel I was impressed by its architectural gems. Handsome Italianate buildings, pale green, mustard yellow, dusty rose or powder blue, crowned the streets piled high with snow. Anything built before the Revolution in 1917 was superb.

In my travels over Europe I had marveled at the memorable houses of worship I visited, but nothing prepared me for the utter beauty, opulence and glory of St. Isaacs's church in St. Petersburg. Very much smaller in size and more intimate, elaborately decorated in blue and gold, the church possessed majestic columns that

I Remember Chesterfield

supported the domed rotunda where icons of long faced saints seemed to float among gold stars and blue heaven. I was more deeply moved when our leader Michael informed me, "There are no seats in Russian churches except for royalty. Imagine standing for a two hour service immersed in the magnificent sacred Russian choral music. In the flickering candlelight you'd believe these haunting soulful eyes of the saints actually moved."

A far cry, I thought, from the austere synagogue of Chesterfield.

On the same afternoon we visited the small, squat cell where with its low ceiling and dirt floor Dostoevsky had been imprisoned for eight months. I was so sickened by the site and idea I left the tour and waited outside in the clear, cold sunshine.

A pleasant older man, clean-shaven and with piercing blue eyes like luminescent steel, dared to come toward me. "Where do you come from?" He spoke English well.

"The United States."

He was so delighted at my answer. He just stood there smiling. I watched the expression on his face, the longing, admiration, pleasure as though he had miraculously touched a part of his Goddess – America? – he once knew and would never see again or the closest he would ever come to a dream he had long nourished.

More than in the other cities, several things in St. Petersburg bothered me. I saw only a scattering of old men sitting idly in the park. Many young men in military uniform. Nobody strolled the streets or stopped to chat but marched somberly, eyes straight ahead. More big black limousines with drawn shades obviously conveying special privileged Soviet personnel. Drinking water so brown I brushed my teeth in bottled water. Hefty women with huge bellies bloated from too much bread, potatoes and cabbage. Only the red cheeked chubby children, well dressed, laughed and played in their outdoor classes. The Soviets favored their children.

Although I was annoyed at the irregularities and inconveniences of Soviet conditions, I must confess that this, my first trip to Russia, endowed me with extraordinary rewards.

We were treated to a feast of Russian culture not usually offered. In the small, choice Kremlin museum we were privileged to view and gape at the famous collection of fabulous, exquisite Faberge eggs, so elegantly and elaborately conceived and decorated. A chronological series of Queen Catherine's gorgeous Court gowns. A magnificent display of Russian silver and other antiquities. The Tretriakov Museum was a gem although the hawk-eyed women guards gave us little space and watched our every move. I was surprised to discover that Russian artists had enjoyed their own fine school of Impressionism. Of course, what museum can compare to the Hermitage, the highlight of all? I remember the broad palatial sweep of the marble staircase at the entrance, the assembly of 24 Rembrandts hung side by side, the absolutely stunning room completely fashioned of green malachite, and gallery after gallery of worldly treasures of art.

One evening I shunned a banquet and attended a performance of *Rigoletto* at the 6,000 seat Kremlin auditorium. The tenor sang in Italian. The rest of the cast, typical of European countries that prefer to present opera in their own language, sang in Russian. How does one successfully translate the full-bodied vocal sounds of a Verdi or Puccini opera, which I heard in Odessa, into the heavy sounding Russian? ("*Nyet, nyet.*") In Leningrad we listened to an excellent concert by their resident orchestra and we also attended a splendid performance of *Giselle*, danced by the Kirov Ballet.

When I remarked to Tanya, our guide, that I was so impressed by the intricate wood lattice decorations overlaid with gold that I saw in many buildings she replied, "We have an excellent Minister of Culture. When the Germans occupied our land they stabled their horses in our most elegant homes and edifices. Now, we are carefully restoring everything. After all, it's our inheritance."

Somehow I had always considered Russia in a European context but on this trip I realized how much the Orient had influenced the country. I particularly enjoyed the beauty of the churches, the ones the Soviets didn't destroy, their graceful turrets, their joyful use of bright colors, mostly imperial, and the hundreds of icons depicting the elongated faces of sorrowful saints. So much beauty, so much opulence, so much fine art, music and dance of the former Russia the Soviets now treasured and enjoyed. I was grateful to see what we did. I felt so enriched.

Another enormous thrill of the trip came about with the unexpected experience of being catapulted back to my youth. As if a fairy had waved her wand and I found myself not in memory but in actual scenes. In Odessa we sat on long benches to eat at long tables. I saw myself once again in Chesterfield, in Grandpa's summer dining room, bright sunlight streaming through the windows, eating

I Find my Russian Roots

one of Aunt Rose's delicious custards or Grandma's fresh cottage cheese and sour cream.

The small groups of elderly men I glimpsed in the parks wore the same heavy wool visored caps and the same ankle length thick black overcoats as the elderly men I knew as a child. I saw myself clothed in the same kind of outfit I wore in the fifth grade when I spied young girls walking home from school. They could have been my classmates. Again and again I came across actual scenes, recognized people's faces, and noticed styles of dress that hadn't changed in the long years gone by.

At the end of the tour, I was ready to go home. I had eaten all the caviar and chewy black bread I wanted. I had tasted the too sweet, drippy fruit syrups and chopped egg appetizers, duplicates of what Mama had cooked. I spurned kasha and the fish and potato soup my stepfather Joe concocted. That I would not eat then or now.

However, it was on the last day of this emotional journey to Russia that I experienced one of the most monumental, meaningful incidents of my whole life. Something I had been searching for subconsciously all the trip.

About five o'clock in the darkened afternoon I left the *Europa Hotel* to saunter down the busy, bustling *Nevesky Prospekt*. I just wanted to be alone, to lose myself in the city, to observe its inhabitants, to drink the last drops of Russian culture. I wanted to reinforce my memories of where my people had lived, how they had survived, what I thought they had bequeathed me. I often thought of Chesterfield and compared what I had remembered.

Night fell early. Now, at the end of the workday hundreds of people were scrambling to get home. Bus after bus, jammed with

I Remember Chesterfield

bodies, doors barely shut, rolled past me in rapid succession. Last minute shoppers crowded into the food market, GASTRONOMICS, where I witnessed clerks wrap fresh fish in newspapers. I stepped into a bakery. Wonderful smells of newly baked bread and glass cases filled with extravagant pastries, not cheap. When I transposed rubles into American dollars, each cake cost $5. I had been told the ordinary proletariat earned only 28 rubles a month. Into a spacious bookstore I wandered but there was nothing in English. On the street again in the large store windows I gazed at displays of ponderous wooden furniture and shapeless women's dresses and coats, unattractive and expensive. And then I found the department store my fellow travelers had told me not to miss. I entered.

    Several small stalls juxtaposed but with high walls between had scrimpy piles of merchandise stacked on shelves behind their counters, not easy to steal. Terrible quality. Imitation leather. I dawdled along slowly noting the variety of goods until I spied a stall featuring kettles. A whole array of big, old fashioned aluminum kettles just like the one that hummed on the back of Grandma's stove. I was ecstatic. I hadn't seen one since she died in 1932. Now another link with Chesterfield was established. I wanted to buy a kettle but it would have been too clumsy for me to carry home. After admiring the lavish and colorful display of children's toys I walked outside thinking about how often on this trip my emotions had soared or plummeted in disbelief and pity at the stringent, impoverished conditions I had witnessed.

    It began to snow, a gentle snow. Big, lazy flakes, drifting down slowly and steadily dotted my hair and my dark coat like polka dots. I stopped and stood in the circle of bright light under a street

I Find my Russian Roots

lamp. This is my land, I thought, my collective past. I've seen my childhood, even to the middy blouses the girls wore. My history in the faces of men and women. I've eaten their foods, my foods of long ago. I shivered in the ruthless cold. Here lie my roots because my people in America, in Chesterfield, were like these people. No formal education. They labored with their hands, their hearts. Their hardships and sacrifices provided the gifts I thrived on. Their guts, their intelligence, their resourcefulness, their dreams. Their courage sings in my blood.

As I stood there I had the strangest feeling. As though the spirits of my ancestors had clustered behind me. Stout matrons still wearing the wigs they donned at their weddings. Dressed in black silk or fine wool, heavy gold jewelry gleaming on their chests. Full bearded gentlemen, stooped and pale from years of religious study. Rosy cheeked young cousins with dark curly hair and flirtatious eyes. Serious lads. Fat babies. I sensed them all.

"I've come back," I spoke to them in silence. "The only one of your descendants in America who cared enough to make this trip. I wanted to find you and now that I know you, I've come full circle. From you to me to them and back to you. Do you realize how excited I am to see the very soil in which my roots were planted? Do you, can you, my cherished ancestors, know what absolutely enthralls me? Here, in your homeland, I have realized who I am. I am the embodiment of your dreams, the fulfillment of your loving hopes. Listen, my grandfathers, my grandmothers. I am the most fortunate of all. I am an American, a Russian heiress rich in Jewish tradition, educated in freedom. Your blood is my blood. You bequeathed me

I Remember Chesterfield

the inheritance. America has blessed me with the freedom to choose, to love, to live as I see myself."

Into the circle of light a woman in a black coat and hat stepped and broke my reverie. I presumed she was asking directions.

"I'm an American," I answered her smiling. "Americanski. You understand? America. United States," I spoke with pride. She turned and left abruptly.

How could I ever explain to her how wonderful it was to be an American? I stood there, snow swirling softly, alone in the bright light. My tears fell.

So grateful was I to all my forebears, so thankful to the foresight of my great grandfather Harris Kaplan who brought his family out of the oppressive Tsarist regime to the small hamlet of Chesterfield. So grateful to my father who had the courage and stamina to leave Russia and bless me with his love and concern.

The Living End
Chapter XXI

On a lovely late spring day somewhere in the early 1980's I drove back to Chesterfield.

Only a few years ago I had sold the remaining acreage of Mama's little farm which Isi had bequeathed to me to the same developer who had acquired Moe's 90 acres (that he inherited from Mama and where Mrs. Wickson lived.) I was curious to see what the developer had accomplished.

The ride from Hartford to Salem on the new four lane divided highway was a breeze. I bypassed Devil's Hopyard and Witch Meadow, now a State Park, and swung right onto the old two-lane highway, Route 85. Three miles further I slowed down and came upon the entrance to the developer's enclave, Silver Springs, the tract of land Isi had wanted to call Random Rock Acres.

Entering the recently paved winding road I noticed a few Colonial styled homes with neatly cropped lawns not yet landscaped. Alas. As far as I could see the developer had cleared all the area, now a gentle rolling stretch of land. I was horrified. Where were the sunny meadows fragrant with grasses, bayberry and clover? ... Destroyed. The rare grove of cedar trees Isi was so proud of ... obliterated. All the tangled shrubs and crowded trees, the brush and insidious poison ivy ... wiped out. I searched for my landmark, the queenly oak tree ... nowhere visible. The seductive spreads of lush blueberries I so gladly loved to cull ... eradicated. I was so sick at heart, angry, dismayed. How could the developer have been so callous? How could he have deliberately raped the earth of so much natural beauty?

Back on the highway I observed where the Cohens had lived. Their house had been demolished and now four pristine white stately homes ran down the hill in an imposing row, like a scenic postcard of somewhere. Anywhere.

Mama's big house, now rented, still occupied Savin's Corners but the barn across the way had collapsed.

Turning left onto the narrow lane I noticed a single Colonial house stood on the lot were Mama had raised her vegetables. Crowded in its limited space the new house seemed uncomfortable, too close to the lane it faced and overwhelming Mama's adjacent little historic 18th century dwelling which the owner had painted a rich toned early American red. I paused for a moment remembering the many summers I had spent there.

Now I wanted to see the little brook of our courtship. I longed to stand once again on its banks, watch the clear water rush down over the tumbled boulders in its path, swirl and eddy, foam and sing its own sweet song as it raced on its journey. To my surprise and chagrin the approach was boarded up! There was no opening where I could squeeze through to recapture, to savor a nostalgic moment. Annoyed and disappointed, I turned sharp right and drove past Bond's meticulously maintained property to come out on the highway again. I could see that the Schwartz farm up the road no longer existed. Mr. Schwartz had been a stocky, round bellied-man whose family had also kept summer boarders. I smiled as I remembered Bess recounting a childish prank. "There was a wedding at Schwartz's place and we kids had not been invited. But Butch, Moe and I went anyhow. We climbed through a window and no one chased us away."

The gate to the Kosofski's delightful brook I had enjoyed so often was locked and their house, set far back, appeared desolate. At the next corner the one room schoolhouse which both my mother and Isi had attended had been swallowed up and transformed into a modern Fire Station sporting a sign out front, "BINGO EVERY SATURDAY NIGHT".

On the corner the house where Aunt Doris and Uncle Jake had resided was converted to a nondescript motel. Close by, the huge front windows of Aunt Helen's store, which had been sold, were completely plastered with several cheap, gaudy advertisements.

When I drove up the long hill toward New London, past the artificial brick faced apartment house, once the dance hall, I knew that off to my right on the Flanders Road only a few charred timbers lay in the grass where the little synagogue, the center of the Russian Jewish community, had flourished. I didn't approach it but drove straight up the hill. At its crest the house that belonged to Grandpa's brother Isaac and his wife Lena had been extended and modified into a few small shops.

Now I turned the car around, went back down the hill and at its bottom, to the left, I entered the lane I recall as shady and deeply rutted. In seconds I drove up the short steep hill to my grandparents' home. I had not been back since 1932 when Grandma died and I never learned to whom my mother sold the property after Grandpa left. There wasn't a single piece of wood lying anywhere around. The whole house which I can reconstruct in my mind so vividly, the well enclosure, ice house, wash house, shabby barns, chicken coop, even

I Remember Chesterfield

the six room cabin at the far end of the orchard had been razed and cleared away. The barbed wire fencing under which I had so deftly scooted was gone. No longer did the wooden fence protect what had been the vegetable garden and grape arbor. And every one of the old gnarled apple trees where we had swung lazy summer hours away had been uprooted and destroyed. Only a lonesome wind blew over the empty, grassy top of the plateau. Not a vestige, not a trace, not a tangible stick remained of the happy wonderful times I had spent in my youth with my grandparents. I was so heartbroken, so appalled; the nothingness choked me. I couldn't even get out of the car to inhale once again the sweet smelling country air.

Sadly I headed for home. Coming to Chesterfield had been a distressing and disturbing experience. I had known about some of the changes, the conversions that had transpired in Chesterfield, like the Fire Station and dance hall, but I had not realized, had not been aware of all the drastic differences that had taken place in the last 50 years. So clear and strong had my memories of former times remained.

But as I neared home my mood lifted. I came into the house, flung my coat over a chair and walked directly to the breakfront where Mama's hand-wrought candlesticks, well over 250 years old, and Grandma's Majolica salad plate were displayed. I picked up the miniature picture of her and gazed at her young, pretty face. It was an early photograph. Her abundant dark hair was coiled in a topknot. Her skin unblemished and white, her eyes already patient. She stood erect, not as I remember her stooped in later years.

"It's all gone, Grandma." I spoke to her softly. "Everybody. Everything. Nothing's left. All that you Russian Jewish farmers built in

Chesterfield with the help of Baron de Hirsch is no more. The small, precious slice of American history you created with your hearts, your sweat, your determination and honest ideals is now legend.

You were the pioneers, the generation lost in transition from one land to another. But your legacy lives on. You sent your sons and daughters and their descendants into America where they still weave threads into the splendid fabric that is our country.

I don't know what relics, what mementos any descendants of all the Jewish people who once lived in Chesterfield now possess. I know that legal, dry statistics are recorded in Montville. But I remember the simple life, Grandma, the little *shul,* the natural lush beauty of the land, the humble people who walked with God. I remember all of this, Grandma."

"I remember Chesterfield."

I Remember Chesterfield

Site of the
Chesterfield Synagogue
1892 – 1975

As early as 1890, Chesterfield was one of three Connecticut communities (Ellington and Colchester the others) chosen by the Baron Maurice de Hirsch Fund of New York to resettle Eastern European Jews seeking refuge from religious persecution.

On May 6, 1892, several Russian Jewish immigrant families living in and around Chesterfield, having incorporated themselves as the New England Hebrew Farmers of the Emanuel Society, consecrated a modest one room synagogue on this site. The purpose of the Society was recorded as follows in the Town of Montville Land Records:

> We, the subscribers, for the purpose of perpetuating the cause of Judaism in all its essential purity, and cherishing and promoting its great and fundamental principle in the Rock upon which our undying Faith is founded, the belief in and worship of one God, hereby unite to form a Society for public worship according to the principles and practices of our Faith.

For over fifty tears, the synagogue flourished as a vibrant religious and social center for the Jewish people of Chesterfield. To preserve and honor their memory, their dreams, struggles and achievements, we their descendants lovingly dedicate this historic marker.

September 28, 1986   24 Elul, 5746

The Montville Becentennial Commision
The Conneticut Historical Commision
The American Jewish Historical Society

Chesterfield Synagogue Monument

The Monument
Epilogue

Our daughter Nancy, as did her father before her, possesses a penchant and love for historic places, things and people. Chesterfield is one of them, stemming from the memorable days she spent at Mama's. She treasures the old Russian hand-wrought copper pots and kettle that Mama brought from Russia.

It was her idea about ten years after the little *shul* in Chesterfield burned down in 1975 to preserve that historic acre of land as a permanent tribute to the Chesterfield Jewish farmers who had lived, struggled and died there.

At first she hoped the State of Connecticut would accept the land as a historic site and assume its care and preservation, but it was not possible. Nor did the town of Montville desire to acquire the property and its maintenance.

Ruth Mantak, my friend and an attorney, asked me, "What do you really want to do with the land?"

"Keep it," I answered her, "in perpetuity so no commercial developer, no hot dog stand or condominiums can ever obliterate its historic and sentimental value."

"Then reactivate the New England Hebrew Farmers Society," she said, "It's never been terminated. It still exists."

We did just that. We selected willing officers and a Board of Trustees. I wrote to as many descendants as I could find asking them for donations to clear the land and erect a monument. Nancy made all the arrangements.

I Remember Chesterfield

On September 28, 1986 at 4 o'clock on a lovely sunny fall afternoon, about 100 people, young and old, assembled for the dedication. Aunt Rosie's son Bernard Saul flew in from California with his wife Ruth. Aunt Mollie's son, Alfred Meisner, and his wife Shirley drove up from Washington, D.C. Mindy Kaplan, formerly of New London came from Florida with her husband and daughter. Ben Kaplan and Rebecca Shragowitz, both 97 years old, who had been in the same class at school attended as well as a new born baby boy a month old.

The program for the dedication was impressive and heart warming. Tears crept into my eyes when Cantor Arthur S. Koret of the Emanuel Synagogue, West Hartford, sang the *Ayl Moly Rochamin*, the prayer for the dead. Andrew Aldrich, representing The Town of Montville which was celebrating its Bicentennial, brought greetings. Jack Shanahan, the Executive Director of the Connecticut Historical Commission, stated that Nancy's effort to establish this memorial, "has given a new light to a unique part of the state's history. An important chapter of the Connecticut history will not be lost." Congressman Sam Gejdenson was detained in Chicago but New York State Senator Pankin reminisced about his father Hayyim who was the first Jewish settler in Chesterfield in 1890. He wooed several disgruntled Russian Jewish immigrants out of the big city to come to Chesterfield. Such bargains were to be had and he needed 10 men for a *minyan*.

Standing only a few feet from the charred timbers on the ground, the handsome monument, six feet tall, five feet wide, fashioned of Mt. Rushmore granite, was unveiled. Its bold bronze plaque displays the story.

Dr. Bernard Wax, Executive Director of the American Jewish Historical Society, spoke. "In many ways the story of Chesterfield, the synagogue and its inhabitants, is the story of acculturation to America. For many of us it is our own story or of our parents. When we mark this day, we honor not only the synagogue but the people in the community, both Jewish and non Jewish who welcomed them."

"They left a legacy of honest toil, the dignity of labor and the concept of self help."

Most interesting to me were some of the comments I heard. Ben Kaplan reflected on the exodus of the early settlers who failed and left. "Russian Jews," he said, "were not farmers."

"It was pretty hard to eke out a living in Chesterfield from a farm," my brother-in-law Butch once said. "We made do between the rocks."

And my sister-in-law Bess summed up the whole picture. "The work ethic stayed with those who remained on the farm. There was no TV, no radio, no automobile, no electricity. If there was no kerosene in the lamp we studied by candlelight. We did not consider this a hardship. We didn't know enough to complain, but thought that was the way the world was."

Today, in the silence of history and the drone of passing cars, the monument stands at the junction of Routes 85 and 161.

Each summer we cut the brush and trim back the trees that spring up.

BIBLIOGRAPHY

Gilbert, Martin, *The Routledge Atlas of Jewish History*. New York: William Morrow and Company Inc., 2002

Klein, Dana L., *To Begin Again: The Russian Jewish Migration to America, with Special Emphasis on Chesterfield, Connecticut*. New London: Connecticut College, 1976

Lee, Samuel J., *Moses of the New World: The Work of Baron de Hirsch*. New York: Thomas Yoseloff, 1970

ABOUT THE AUTHOR

Micki Savin, born in Norwich, Connecticut, earned her B.A. in English Literature at Connecticut College and her M.A. in English Literature at Trinity College. In 1932 she married Isadore Savin, a native of Chesterfield, Connecticut, a small rural village near New London, where her own maternal great-grand parents settled soon after they arrived in New York from Russia in the 1887. During forty years of marriage, Savin was an active volunteer in the Hartford arts community, serving as president for the Hadassah and Sisterhood of the Emanuel Synagogue, the Connecticut Opera Guild and Friends of the Hartford Ballet. She received the Woman of the Year award from Woman's Auxiliary of B'nai Brith in 1965 and the Connecticut Opera's prestigious Medici Award in October of 2003. Savin has written book reviews and numerous articles, many about her travels abroad, for *The Hartford Courant*. She is still deeply involved with the Connecticut Opera Guild, and is a board member of the Friends of the Bloomfield Library, Micki Savin has two children, Nancy and David, five grandchildren and two great-grandchildren.

Made in the USA
Middletown, DE
03 September 2023